Interesting and novel perspective on management balance between the forces of change and those of continuing operations.

Lew Allyn, Chairman,
Welch Allyn, Inc.

Change Creators & Momentum Maximizers" provides a fresh and insightful description of organizations and their productivity. This book catalyzes fundamental business structure and operations dynamics to yield a clear description and new perspective regarding the process of change within organizations.

Carl E. Bretko, President/COO
DentalEz Group

An interesting and well presented treatise that can be helpful and thought provoking for top management. Since Momentum Maximizers and Change Creators are relatively new terms, they can be useful in managing an organization.

Albert Duval, CEO & Chairman
Hammermill Paper Co (retired)

Author offers a very interesting premise in the way he segments the activities in a business. It's a logical and rational way to differentiate the various drivers that are present.

James Perry, President & CEO
Global Thermoelectric Inc. (Canada)

William Miller has written a rare common sense guide through the jungle of the supply chain to maximize productivity while also driving change. The book is well written and erudite, unusual in management books.

D.E.I. Smyth, Senior Vice President
Corporate & Government Affairs
H.J. Heinz Company

This is a strong concept, present early in the text…unique and well presented. This is a good, no-nonsense book that should be helpful to those that read it.

Writers Showcase Review

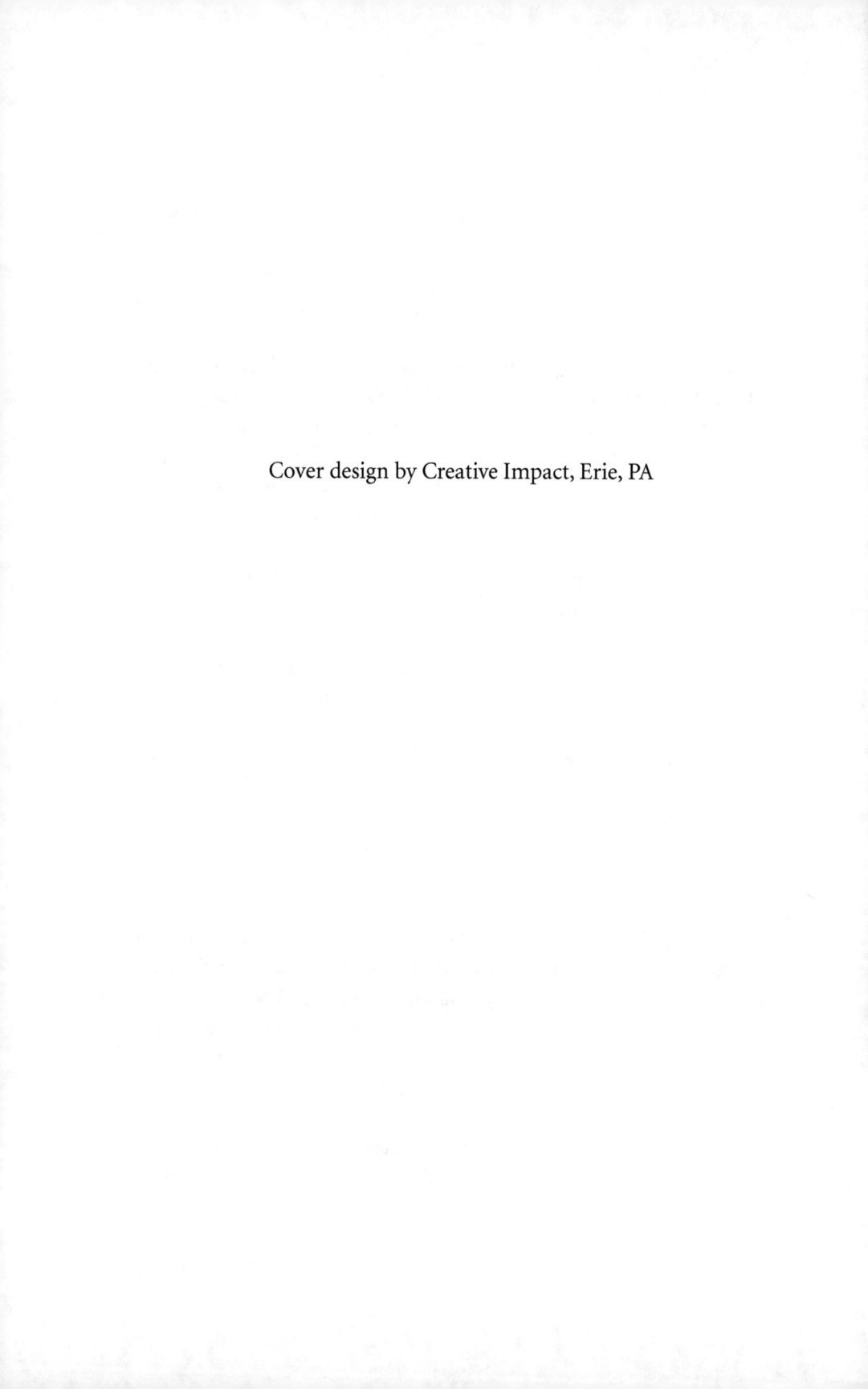

Change Creators and Momentum Maximizers

Change Creators and Momentum Maximizers

William R. Miller

Change Creators and Momentum Maximizers

ISBN: 1-59109-524-7

Printed in the United States of America

Contents

Introduction

It is a major ongoing responsibility of those in management to strive to learn more about the field and measure how well they are succeeding in it. More importantly, they need to determine how that knowledge and understanding can improve their performance. This book endeavors to present another way of looking at the dynamics of business organizations. Although specifics vary, the overall concept presented in this book is equally applicable to government, educational institutions, the military, religious organizations, unions and business…in short, any form of human organization.

You will find, as you read this, that I love quotations and, therefore, will start with two observations that seem to be applicable to management's ongoing need for understanding. To make the point in 700 BC, Homer had one of the gods comment:

> *"Look now how mortals are blaming the gods, for they say that evils come from us, but in fact they themselves have woes beyond their share because of their own follies."*

Some 26 centuries later Pogo condensed this to:

> *"We have met the enemy and he is us."*

This particular book treats, as an example, just one manifestation of the Momentum Maximization & Change Creation concept. It is applied here to business organizations in general and specifically those organizations engaged in manufacture and distribution. (Change Creation and Momentum Maximization manifestations in Government, Education, Religious Institutions and the Military are summarized briefly in Chapter XI).

The main theme will dwell on the categories of activities that have evolved, via a mixture of business theory and trial and error, to where they now appear to characterize the operation of virtually all such businesses. In order to prove the point, I will take the reader on a little tour through a typical manufacturing operation. At each stop, I will attempt to show how every position fits into the overall scheme. (A relatively common organization structure is used here but the basic "building blocks" can be arranged in a number of different ways. The chapter on Organization Development discusses the different ways that an activity can be structured.)

The former standard functional organization titles ("Old Categories") listed below no longer bear much resemblance to the way a modern business is actually run.

"Old Categories"

> President
> Sales
> Engineering
> Manufacturing
> Finance
> Employee Relations

It is the contention of this book that the "New Reality" in which business organizations function is:

New Reality

> Senior Management
> Momentum Maximizers
> Change Creators
> Score Keepers
> Support Suppliers

Further, the major planning and operational task of senior management is to balance these last four strong, and often competing, interest groups for maximum benefit to the company.

Before launching into the analysis of these newly defined groups, it is important from a contextual standpoint, to define or determine the activities that drive their existence.

We will therefore start at what I think of as the beginning of the business logic chain….the "Company's Mission"

I. MISSION

There are already many books and articles on the subject of "Mission" in modern industry so there is little reason to dwell on it here. Simply stated, it is the reason the organization exists, i.e. what it is intended to accomplish, as well as, what is its purpose. It is probably one of the most important formal statements for the management team to agree upon and all employees and suppliers/partners (and yes, all current and prospective competitors as well) understand. Like the Cheshire Cat's observation, "if you don't know where you want to go, then it doesn't matter which way you go", without buy-in on a well thought out and specific Mission for the organization, there is little point in discussing strategic planning and implementation.

On this subject, Barnard, in "The Function of the Executive" observes:

> "Willingness to cooperate, except as a vague feeling or desire for association with others cannot develop without an objective of (such) cooperation. Unless there is a specific objective, it cannot be known what specific efforts will be required of individuals, or in many cases what satisfactions to them can be in prospect. Such an objective we denominate the "purpose" of an organization...A purpose does not incite cooperative activity unless those whose efforts will constitute the organization accept it. Hence there is something like simultaneity in the acceptance of purpose and the willingness to cooperate."

II. STRATEGIC INTENT

This concept appears to be a more recent perception and does not have the documentation trail that Mission enjoys. Intent, as described in current literature, has some of the attributes of a hidden agenda. Missions are frequently a matter of public record, at least in public companies. Even in private companies, the Mission is usually so widely communicated within the organization that it is apparent to outsiders as well.

Strategic Intent, on the other hand, is the confidential guiding principle(s) governing how this management team will achieve the Mission. One of the cited examples in Hamel and Prahalad's article, noted below, is that of the Japanese heavy equipment manufacturer, Komatsu, whose Mission was to be a leader in that market but whose Strategic Intent (as it came out much later) had apparently been, from the very beginning, to "encircle Caterpillar."

It would, therefore, appear that in an ever more sophisticated competitive environment, an organization should think through and bind at least its top or inner circle of management to the Strategic Intent principles that are to be used in carrying out the Mission. I refer the reader to the excellent article on "Strategic Intent" by Hamel and Prahalad that appeared in the Harvard Business Review. It is also covered in the same author's book, "Competing for the Future."

III. STRATEGIC PLAN

Strategic Planning has been well covered in the literature and practices of modern industry. A dynamic, yet consistent plan, a dichotomy in a way, is necessary so that everyone in the organization understands their role - what is required of them, and what they should expect from the others with whom they interact. Like the score of a symphony, the Strategic Plan lays out the who, the what and the when. It is critical that the senior management oversee the evolution of the plan so that it ends up implementing their Strategic Intent without necessarily having it obvious to others, outside that group, what that intent is.

Core Competencies

While on the subject of strategic planning, this is a good place to introduce the concept of "Core Competencies." It is interesting to note how far back the concept of "competencies" as key elements of strategy and planning goes. If Sun Tzu's "Art of War" (~500 BC) were restated into today's business language, certain of the desirable attributes he listed for armies might translate as "competencies." In more recent business literature, Phillip Selznick's 1957 book "Leadership and Administration" used the terms "distinctive competence" to describe the advantage in unique skills a company possessed over those of its competitors and Barnard talks of "limiting (strategic) factors" in much the same vein.

The publications that seem to have most vividly and completely captured and taught the concept of core competency are the HBR article by Hamel and Prahalad "The Core Competence of the Corporation" and their book noted previously. (I understand their reprint is one of the most requested that HBR has ever had. I recommend both publications to the reader). The power of this tool certainly seems to have invigorated the thinking of many business leaders.

I would not venture to condense either of these publications, but for the purpose of understanding how the term is used in this book, I will outline the three "tests" the authors propose to verify the existence of a core competency. The exact wording of the test questions varies somewhat between their article and their book but the concept is the same.

TEST 1.)   Does it provide access to a wide range of markets? (Article)

Does it form the basis for entry into new product markets? (Book)

TEST 2.)   Does it make a significant contribution to the perceived customer benefits of the end product? (Article)

Does it make a disproportionate contribution to customer perceived value? (Book)

TEST 3)   Is it difficult for competitors to imitate? (Article)

Is it competitively unique? (Book)

It is very interesting to observe that, when a company "catches the disease" and really begins to examine the costs of trying to maintain in-house competencies that are not "core" to the success of the business, there are some very clear "symptoms."

First, divisions, services and product lines, which are not supported by the current (or planned) competencies of the organization, are divested (or outsourced in the case of some support services). Second, alliances and mergers are aggressively sought with other organizations that possess a competency the company lacks and needs for success, but cannot justify the time and resources to develop in-house.

This is a powerful tool for strategic planning and implementation. It even amazed me, as I wrote this book, how many times the core competency concept showed up as I went through the various parts of a business organization. I feel that Strategic Planning is better matched to modern reality when core competency concepts are rigorously applied and the role assignments are grouped according to the "New Categories" noted previously.

The chapters that follow will discuss these categories and show that they can be a more meaningful way to approach both the plan and the way the organization is structured to carry it out.

IV. SENIOR MANAGEMENT

In his discussion of leaders, Selznick points out, "The relationship of leadership to organizational character may be more closely explored if we examine some of the key tasks leaders are called upon to perform:
    1) The definition of institutional mission and role.
    2) The institutional embodiment of purpose.
    3) The defense of institutional integrity
    4) The ordering of internal conflict. - Internal interest groups form naturally in large-scale organizations, since the total enterprise is in one sense a polity composed of a number of sub-organizations. The struggle among competing interests always has a high claim on the attention of leadership. This is because the direction of the enterprise as a whole may be seriously influenced by changes in the internal balance of power."

We have already touched upon his points (1) and (2) and will cover (3) later. It is his point (4) that emphasizes the balancing role in general and, in particular, the strong competing interests represented by groups like the Momentum Maximizers and the Change Creators.

The management of today's complex organizations requires so much time and such a wide variety of skills, that the senior management of a modern corporation is frequently headed by a management team, each responsible for specific segments of the task assigned. Barnard alludes to this phenomenon when he observes,

"In some cases the executive...may be not a person but a board...a committee. I know of no important organization, except some churches and some absolute governments, in which the highest objective authority is not lodged in an organized executive group, that is, a "highest" unit of organization."

6

In my view, the roles seem to naturally fall in place as follows: (Note that in smaller companies, one individual may be responsible for more than one of these roles, but the roles are still distinct and different.)

Chairman of the Board

This is the job of providing the link between the Board of Directors and the senior management of the company (usually the CEO). This "linking" is inherent when the Chairman and CEO jobs are held by the same individual.

With outside Directors increasingly being held personally responsible for actions of the company in many areas, the Chairman's job has radically changed. It is no longer just presiding over quarterly meetings where the recommendations of senior management were frequently routinely endorsed. The involvement of the members of the Board has, in most cases, become deeper and more frequent. The Chairman must constantly coordinate with, communicate to, gain the approval of (proposals, budgets, etc.) and see to the implementation of the decisions of these Board members.

As the head of the Board of Directors, this individual must motivate, educate and provide leadership to the Board in discharging their duties. These duties have now extrapolated from the basic "representing the interests of the stockholders" into strategy, long range business (and senior executive succession) planning, etc.

Chief Executive Officer

Except for those special situations that require Board action (such as removing the CEO) the Chief Executive Officer is "where the buck stops" regarding final decisions and their implementation involving both long term and immediate actions of the company.

There are many sample "Job Descriptions" for CEO's so here is an representative example taken from Coventry and Burstiner's book "Management - A Basic Handbook:"

"(a) Making sure that the objectives, as laid down by the board, are kept well in mind by the whole organization and, where necessary, recommending to the board revisions in those objectives to keep pace with change.

(b) Being actively concerned with long-range planning and strategy, based on a thorough understanding of the main trends in the dynamic environment of the firm. Supervising any changes. e.g. in production, considered necessary.

(c) Ensuring the financial soundness of the company as a whole, with each department, branch or operation making its proper contribution.

(d) Maintaining an effective organizational structure, with the practical effects of growth, including likely changes in key personnel, kept firmly in mind. Building up a strong management team.

(g) Keeping control over the business so that it conforms to the plans laid down.

(h) Providing a high standard of personal leadership and motivating all concerned to give continually of their best."

NOTE: I omitted "e" from the original text since I consider it a "Chief Operating Officer duty" and "(f)" from the original text since I consider it a "Presidential duty." This editing results from separating the CEO, COO and President jobs for purposes of this discussion.

To this comprehensive listing of CEO duties, I would propose to add: (i) Balancing the resources available between the Momentum Maximizers and the Change Creators to provide growth and timely reaction to changing conditions on the one hand while maintaining the strength of the underlying business so that it can continue to generate the wealth required to fund the enterprise."

President

The President represents the company to the outside world including the communities in which the company does business, the other companies in the same business sector (often through trade associations, etc.), government agencies at all levels, the financial community, the financial analysts of a public company, major customers and partners, the media, and so on.

Chief Operating Officer

The Chief Operating Officer is responsible for running the company on a day-to-day, moment-to-moment basis. It is a "downward focused" job whose main concern is operating the organization in the most effective and efficient manner possible. This would include balancing the immediate resource needs of the Momentum Maximizers and the Change Creators (and their respective support organizations), resolving operational conflicts, problem resolution, business tactics, etc.

General Manager (decentralized profit center)

As companies grew larger, many elected to break up the business into smaller, more easily managed separate businesses headed by "para" senior managers carrying the title "General Manager," Division Vice President, etc. When it is necessary to resort to decentralization, the need for a strong common understanding is an even more critical prerequisite. Selznick puts it: "The need for centralization declines as the homogeneity of personnel increases. A unified outlook, binding all levels of administration, will permit decentralization without damage to policy."

Typically, the General Manager has his (or her) dedicated Momentum Managers and Change Creators and those Score Keepers and Support Suppliers who are needed by them on a day-to-day basis. Normally, the major Score Keeper and Support Supplier personnel assigned to a General Manager have a dual reporting arrangement in that they also report to the Senior Executives responsible for that activity at the corporate level, e.g. VP Finance, VP Human Resources, etc.

Selznick takes note of this dilemma at some length.

> *"Let us apply this idea to the classical headquarters-field problem. Given a headquarters organization and a field organization, to whom shall subject matter specialists...be responsible? To the technical staff chief at headquarters or to the head of the local field organization? The dilemma is that the headquarters staff will be concerned over values (e.g. good accounting procedure), but the field executive will be under pressure to get an immediate job done while perhaps taking insufficient account of the long run consequences of his decisions. One answer has been "dual supervision" in which certain officers are thought of as "administratively" responsible to one superior while "technically" responsible to another...But "dual supervision" really presumes an optimum situation in which a strong, value-oriented elite (the technical staff) has had enough autonomy to lay down professional criteria that are accepted by the line officials."*

It is much less common that the Marketing, R.D.&E., or Manufacturing people assigned would have such dual reporting arrangements.

As noted in the section on community relations, in these days of geographically dispersed operations, it is unlikely there will be a member of the parent company's senior management in residence. It then falls upon the senior, local General Manager to represent the corporation to the community in addition to his or her operational duties.

I can't leave the subject of Senior Management without a quote from Machiavelli and a current day example of his point:

"Therefore a prince (read CEO), …if he is wise he ought not to fear the reputation of being mean, for in time he will come to be more considered than if liberal, seeing that with his economies his revenues are enough,…and (he) is able to engage in enterprises without burdening his people; thus it comes to pass that he exercises liberality toward all from whom he does not take, who are numberless, and meanness toward those to whom he does not give, who are few."

This point of view was brought home to me very graphically in the case of a company that had temporarily come into some difficult times. Unfortunately, for those involved, it seems that the CEO at the time was a "very nice guy." He, as a result, apparently couldn't bring himself to take the drastic actions necessary that would have affected a relatively small number of people (whose outplacement or reassignment could still have been handled on a fair and professional basis). Instead, his failure to be a little, selectively, (and in my view necessarily) "mean" brought down the whole company and negatively impacted the lives of hundreds or maybe thousands of people.

I'm with Machiavelli…heaven protect us from "nice" CEO's in tough times.

V. MOMENTUM MAXIMIZERS

Having set the stage with the planning and outlining of senior management roles, we can now turn to the first of the new lineup of de facto organizations in American business...the Momentum Maximizers. These are the people, throughout the organization, whose main goal is to achieve the best possible results, for the longest possible time, with no major change in products, organization, or processes.

For instance, the same basic distribution channels are used, the same technologies are employed in the same products, the same manufacturing processes and facilities are employed, etc.

Many strategic plans utilize a "Momentum Line" in their long-range forecasts to indicate the probable trend if the business were to continue without change in areas such as those cited. The Momentum Maximizers are the ones in the organization who are responsible for the activities that sustain this ongoing part of the business.

This is not to imply that the Momentum Maximizers do not make any changes at all. However, the adjustments they make (to keep things running) do not alter the fundamental characteristics of the business. An analogy might be the "static adaption" made by individuals. Erich Fromm defines "By static adaption we mean such an adaption to patterns as leaves the whole character structure unchanged and implies only the adoption of a new habit. By dynamic adaption we refer to the kind of adaption...(that) creates something new in him, arouses new drives." Note that the change creators (discussed later) are involved in the equivalent of Fromm's "dynamic adaption."

One of the few situations in which Momentum Maximizing has high distinct visibility is when, for one reason or another, it is vital to make the bottom line look good quickly at all costs. One way this result can be achieved is by getting rid of all the "Change Creators" and their associated support (and other related discretionary spending). What remain are only the Momentum Maximizers and their support.

Here the Momentum Maximizers' efforts are visible as the sole results that the company achieves, without the costs of funding the Change Creators. The bottom line should initially improve dramatically. However, using this technique in the longer run, the organization will probably eventually be out of business. (In some instances "making money on the way out of the business" may have been the intent all along).

In the vast majority of companies involved in distribution and manufacturing the Momentum Maximizers can be categorized into three main groupings; Sales, Product Engineering and Production. These are supported by elements of "The Score Keepers" and "The Support Suppliers" who are both discussed later. The emphasis in all of the Momentum Maximizers is on such things as improving efficiency, ROA, effectiveness, and product/service quality. Their measurements of performance reflect their focus on these areas.

The following chapters that discuss the various manifestations of Momentum Maximization are not intended to describe in detail all the activities that take place. The discussion is more intended to give the reader a "flavor" of Momentum Maximization. Since this section on momentum deals with an ongoing business, with a history, with existing products going to existing markets, we will begin where all such activity is triggered...in Sales.

SALES

In this chapter we will group under "sales" all the activities that take place on an order for goods or services up to and including the physical receipt of the order, with the exception of the Product Engineering portion (which is discussed later).

Since we are dealing with existing organizations, it is presumed that all the components of this sales definition are in place in one form or another. The following illustrates some of the more typical parts of this "Sales" activity.

    1. Distribution
        a. Direct sales
        b. Distributor/dealer sales
        c. Representatives
        d. Domestic
        e. International
    2. Contract & Quotation
    3. Order processing
    4. Credit
    5. Advertising
    6. Customer Service
    7. Order forecast
    8. Warehousing
    9. Sales information security

Distribution

The core of the sales effort is the distribution arrangement. There is a great deal in literature about the trade-offs between direct sales, distributors and the use of representatives ("reps") so that discussion will not be repeated here. Suffice to say that the combination chosen must be related to such factors as the type of product, the type of market, the position of the organization within those markets, synergy with products of other divisions (in a multi-division/business company). Recall that, in the selection of channels, momentum maximization requires extracting the most income producing sales from the chosen channels at minimum expense while maintaining the sales infrastructure base for the future. Tactically, an important consideration in making distribution decisions is also the distribution strategy of the major competitors.

For instance, direct sales generally work well with a smaller, but very focused customer base. If you have an opportunity for relatively few transactions of high dollar value per order, you will be more likely to be successful in a direct sales situation.

In direct sales, it is important to quantify the potential of each territory, by product if possible, in sales dollars and margin dollars, and then measure (and strive to improve) the attainment. At the same time commission expense, travel and entertainment outlays must be controlled, all the while holding personnel turnover to a reasonable level.

Distributor sales involve such considerations as: determining the type and quantity of support from the organization that the distributors require for most cost effective results; the degree of territory overlap and duplication to get good coverage; providing sufficient exclusivity to make the line attractive to desirable distributors; the amount and conditions for the distributor discount from list; the qualification (and requalification) of distributors; stocking requirements; credit capability; etc. One also needs to measure the amount of influence on brand selection that the dealer possesses, i.e., how much leverage does the distribution channel have with the end user in terms of product selection?

Manufacturer's representatives (reps) who work on commission, carry no inventory (and normally, no receivables) are another mode of distribution widely employed. Manufacturers with a narrow product line offering, selling a specialized product into a market that buys a far wider range of products, frequently employ "reps" as the most cost effective way to reach their market.

The arrangements for international distribution involve all the same factors as domestic plus the added complication of political and economic considerations.

Managing the distribution portion of Sales is, therefore, a balancing act. The individual in charge must be highly focused on fine-tuning the channel to get "the most bang for the buck." It is particularly critical in dealing with sales management that "marching orders" be clear and unambiguous. Imposing conflicting requirements and measurements on this position will usually lead to sub-optimization of results.

We shall see that many of the activities in the general area of momentum maximization require similar resource/results "balancing skills."

Contract and Quotation

The Contract and quotation part of the sales function obviously varies considerably with the type of product. For the "standard" catalog-type item it may be only determining model numbers and putting out the price sheets regularly.

It is in the case of "specials" that this function has an expanded role. Where all products are essentially specials, which is typical of the systems business, the contract and quotation function is a vital operational activity. Customer requirements must be completely and quickly identified, product engineering and production scheduling coordinated, arrangements made for any outside make items required to fill out the package, and a timely and accurate response given to the potential customer. If it entails a complex system, it is not unusual for this function to also have the responsibility for shepherding the order through manufacture, delivery, installation and startup.

Order Processing

Order processing in Sales is, hopefully, self-explanatory. It includes order acknowledgement, checking with Credit, converting the order into a format that Production (and Product Engineering if involved) can understand and utilize, etc.

Credit

Credit, in the domestic market, has become much more straightforward over the years. There are so many sources for assessing a domestic customer's financial situation that a well-run company really has few excuses for mistakes in this area.

It is in the international arena that the credit function has to earn its keep. In much of the world, hard currency is difficult to come by. Too often the main questions are not price and delivery, but rather, "what does the customer have in mind as far as paying for the product?" The unsung heroes of the steady improvement in U.S. exports, particularly to countries other than the so-called developed countries, may be the sophisticated credit managers in the successful exporting companies. The Customer Service function and the Credit function for international business typically function as one team. In many companies the manager of the Credit function and the international Customer Service function are the same individual.

Advertising

Although Advertising is obviously also involved as a tool in the introduction of new products and services (see the Change Creators), it is probably even more central as a tool of Sales to sustain the momentum of the existing products. Even when depicting a new product, Advertising is supporting the traditional products by maintaining the visibility and image of the entire organization. In addition to visibility, Advertising has major tasks in imbuing new excitement into older products, in generation of leads, and in sending "messages" to customers, stockholders and competitors. For all of these reasons, it has been included as an activity of the Sales portion of the Momentum Maximizers.

One of the most cost effective ways to reach customers for leads has evolved from utilizing non-face-to-face techniques such as telemarketing and the Internet. With the high cost of fielding sales people, companies today focus on increasing the amount of time the sales person has in front of a "pre-qualified" customer rather than just going in on a regular call pattern and assuming the customer can induced to be "interested in something." Telemarketing and more recently, the Internet are tools to accomplish this aim and have therefore become important parts of the Sales function. They are really related to advertising in this role since one of their principle purposes is to uncover qualified leads.

Customer Service

Although it may be organizationally placed under another heading, Customer Service deserves identification as a distinct Sales activity. Due in no small part to the structure of commission plans, sales makers are highly focused individuals and that focus is normally on getting the order and then moving on to the next opportunity. A whole different "personality" is needed to maintain continuity with the customer on any particular order from entry through warranty. Except for large systems jobs, with dedicated project managers, as mentioned previously, the impression the customer has of the organization is heavily influenced by their opinion of the customer service function.

Order Forecasting

Modern manufacturing techniques with their MRP, JIT, etc. have made order forecasting an extremely important part of Sales' role in the Momentum Maximizing effort. This will be discussed in more length in the Production Planning and Inventory Control sections of the discussion of the Production function.

Warehousing

Warehousing may not necessarily fall under Sales organizationally, but it is clearly part of the Sales armamentarium. Remote warehouses normally exist to improve quality of sales response to orders for stock products. This may involve reduction in shipping time and cost, avoidance of delays at border customs, dealer support, disaster protection, etc. Maintaining such facilities is clearly costly in terms of both expense and inventory and therefore, normally used sparingly.

Sales Information Security

Sales information security is discussed here because it is too frequently underemphasized. Sales makers tend by nature to be gregarious, open people. Coincidentally, some of the most important bits of information needed for modern, competitor-based strategic planning is data on the volume and makeup of the sales (and the sales stratagems) of all the players in a given market (subjects about which people in the sales function are conversant). This is a combination filled with risk and deserves visibility on a par with that traditionally associated with security of proprietary technical data.

Sales Summary

These are the principle components of the Sales sub-team of the Momentum Maximizers team. Of all the sub-teams that will be discussed, this Sales group is usually the tightest knit, with very close interpersonal ties business-wise as well as socially.

PRODUCT ENGINEERING

Product Engineering is the technical sub-team of the Momentum Maximizers team. As such, it is responsible for the integrity of the product design and its documentation, be it standard product or special. Since measurements will be touched upon, it is assumed that all technical personnel account for their time against projects, products, orders, generic categories, etc. Further, this time is converted into cost using an hourly rate in order that the costs in the activity can be measured.

As noted in the section on Scorekeepers, it was Lord Kelvin who pointed out that if you can't measure something you don't know very much about it. That certainly applies to the use of engineering resources. I had originally planned to include the article that I wrote on this subject a number of years ago in an Appendix. It contained a discussion of approaches and guidelines for calculating such engineering liquidation rates. I am concerned that it may be somewhat dated, so I have just included a reference to the article in the Bibliography.

The Product Engineering sub-team has two major branches and these branches share some common responsibilities.

Current Products

The first branch is "Current Products Engineering." This is the day-to-day technical work that must be done to sustain a product in production. Much of this work involves engineering changes, i.e., implementation of cost improvements, substitution for discontinued components, and, on an evolutionary basis, improved manufacturability and quality, etc. (The concept of "static adaption" cited previously).

Every proposed engineering change must be reviewed to make sure that there is no inadvertent change in the function, appearance or interchangeability of the product. Current products engineering is both the guardian of the design integrity of the product and the custodian of the evolutionary adjustments that must be made in a dynamic environment.

Current products engineering is also accountable for the security of the technical documentation of all the products that are either in production or which were in production as far back as the organization wishes to (or is mandated by law to) provide service and support. (In order to do this they must be able to accurately reconstruct the revision level at any time of manufacture of any of these products.) Provision must be made to keep the design documentation safe, secure and available in the event of a disaster that wipes out the documentation currently in use in production and/or service.

Since current products engineering is really part of the ongoing cost of making the product it is frequently charged into manufacturing overhead or burden. As a percent of manufacturing cost it can be tracked and targeted for continuous improvement as part of the organizations effort to improve results.

Custom Engineering

The other branch of Product Engineering is called "requisition engineering," or "custom engineering," or "system engineering," or similar designation. It is the engineering function that is concerned with the engineering and documentation of "specials." Specials are non-standard versions or combinations of the standard product sometimes combined with specially procured, outside sourced components. As noted, some organizations have no "specials" and don't require this function. Some make nothing but specials and this type of engineering is then a competence that is key to their success. As one might guess, there are many who make a "standard" product, but who also are responsive to customer requests and needs for specials and therefore must also have this capability.

Unlike the current products branch, which can do its work on a scheduled, semi-off-line basis, custom engineering is right in the sales-production loop. When a request for a quote on a special comes in from the field, they must quickly put together a proposed design so it can be costed and production estimated to allow Sales to respond to the customer. If the quote turns into an order, they must translate the proposed design into hard documentation for Production.

One of the main secrets of success in a specials business is good up-front product structuring. The standard product itself must have been designed with the possibility of specials in mind. The arrangement of sub-assemblies, the organization of bills of material, the factory flow, the inventory levels, test and quality control planning should all have been put in place to make specials as painless as possible. (If this has not been done, the processing of specials will have some of the negative impact as the actions of the Change Creators discussed later.)

Since custom engineering is tied to specific special jobs, the cost can be accumulated and charged against that job. In this way all the costs (not just production costs) of a specific order can be captured for measurement. Since this work is a variable tied to the number and complexity of specials, it is more often classified, for accounting purposes, as a direct charge to cost-of-sales.

Both branches of Product Engineering have a responsibility to preserve (at a minimum), but more desirably to strengthen, the core competencies upon which the success of the existing products of the organization depend.

Technical Field Support

The "buck" for Technical field support stops in Product Engineering. If the customer or the distributor/rep can't resolve a field problem, if field sales then can't solve it, if field service can't solve it, if customer service can't solve it…product engineering "has got to solve it." In order to minimize the number of times they have to "drop everything else cause there's trouble in the field," it is incumbent on Product Engineering to perfect ever more trouble-free design improvements. They must also equip all others in the chain with the best training and tools possible to solve it as close to the problem identification point as possible. Reduction in the need for after-sales service and improvement in response, when it is needed, has been a major target of Quality programs for years.

PRODUCTION

Production can be considered the oldest, most established part of the Momentum Maximizers. After some Change Creators designed and built the first "prototype" pyramid at the dawn of history, it was "production" people who built the rest. Some Change Creator may have designed the format, but from then on, the construction of the Great Wall of China was a "production" job.

Assembly line methods date back at least to the third century B.C. when Xenophon observed: "Here a man lives only from sewing the shoes, there another only from cutting them…the simpler the process, the more successful it is." The medieval guilds were production specialization by trade. It is no wonder then that production people are the traditional "seasoned veterans" of the Momentum Maximizers.

Production includes all the folks in the "engine room" of the enterprise. Their role is to translate the orders and/or forecasts from sales into product delivered to a customer at the lowest total cost, in the shortest possible time, and of the highest possible quality. It is perhaps, an even more demanding balancing act than that required of Sales.

A Manager of Manufacturing of a division of a major corporation confided to me that there were so many interdependent measurements imposed on his function that, at any given point in time, there were at least three measurements, on the basis of which, he conceivably could be fired. Now, I recognize that he may have been exaggerating, to some extent, but consider the following.

In order to provide the fastest possible response to new orders, it is best to have finished goods on hand or at least assemblies and sub-assemblies built up to a high "level." This, however, runs contrary to the pressure on keeping inventories at the lowest possible dollar level to maximize inventory turns (critical to high return on assets). Investment in tooling can drive down labor hours, but the resulting depreciation hits the numerator and the capital investment hits the denominator of the important return on assets measurement.

Like Sales, Production consists of a number of complimentary and interrelated departments. The following are some of the more typical parts of this activity.

1. Production Planning & Control
2. Purchasing
3. Receiving
4. Component manufacture
5. Inventory Control
6. Assembly
7. Test
8. Shipping
9. Process Information Security

Production Planning and Control

Production Planning and Control, particularly with the advent of computer scheduling and MRP, JIT, etc. systems, is the nerve center of manufacturing. Production Planning originates the directions to order materials, directs the shop to what, how many, and when to build, etc.

In modern American manufacturing, it is a wonder of efficiency and effectiveness, particularly when the same products are built in the same product matrix pattern over an extended period of time. (One can appreciate that specials and new products can be viewed by Production as injecting poison into this smoothly running system.)

A little appreciated aspect of MRP is that, in one context, it can be viewed as the greatest single "coup" that the Production function ever pulled off on their Sales associates. In the "olden" days, the culture in Sales was to try to get away with the lowest possible orders commitment to the business. Then, when they came in way over, they were hailed as heroes.

With MRP, Sales is required to forecast and the whole manufacturing pipeline is loaded from that forecast with inventories minimized and labor hours balanced. If Sales were "sandbagging" the potential, and orders really came in much higher, Sales would have unhappy customers with missed deliveries and/or the business would pay a premium for rush material and overtime. Sales can no longer be the "over forecast hero." Production has imposed a discipline on sales forecasting to an extent that never existed pre-MRP.

Purchasing

Purchasing is another part of the production area that has undergone a major paradigm shift in recent times. The old image of the cigar-chewing purchasing agent beating down vendors to squeeze the last penny and most unreasonable deliveries from a number of competing companies is largely a thing of the past. The modern procurement professional spends his energy building long- term, close relationships with as small a number of high quality suppliers as possible. The suppliers chosen are those that can operate more like partners in the success of the total business. Both parties must be willing to contribute their share to the success of the venture and expect to participate in the success of the venture.

The wisdom of this approach is reinforced by the recent focus on core competencies and capabilities. Since few, if any, organizations can afford to sustain in-house, all of the competencies required to participate in a given market, the company's internal strengths must be supplemented by strengths derived through permanent arrangements with suppliers/partners that can fill the gaps. Supplier/partners are increasingly reluctant to grant access to their proprietary skill set without a long-term business commitment.

Receiving

Even the "ancient" art of Receiving with examples of documentation which go back to ancient Mesopotamia, is being fine-tuned by the Momentum Maximizers. With focus on return on assets in turn spotlighting inventory reduction, the period between the time material arrives at the receiving dock and the manufacturing (or warehousing) system "recognizes" it is available, represents non-value-added asset utilization time. Some retailers, for example, have gone to the extreme of requiring notice of shipment from the suppliers and then using forecasted transit times to load their inventory. The item shows as available simultaneously with its arrival on the receiving dock. Data collection techniques such as bar coding can speed the process of receipt confirmation and eliminate human error.

Component Manufacture

"To component manufacture, or not to manufacture, that is the question" (to paraphrase Shakespeare). There was a time where vertical integration was the norm. It wasn't called by such a fancy name back then. In the days before the proliferation of specialty suppliers and the materials supply infrastructure, organizations had to make all the components they needed. Even today in the developing nations this is still true. I was involved at one time working in China to set up a modern hospital equipment manufacturing plant. The plant initially had to make everything, even such items like pipe nipples, since there was not an existing network of reliable industrial supply houses.

Decisions on what components (and sub-assemblies) to make in-house are much more complex today. Since one's core competencies are what provide competitive advantage, it usually makes sense to manufacture the components in-house that embody that competence. Conversely, if a particular competence is arranged for through partnership instead, it usually makes sense to procure the components (or sub-assemblies) embodying that competence from that supplier/partner. The extreme of this is probably the case of organizations whose only distinct competence/capability is distribution, where even the products themselves are procured from supplier partners.

It is a hard decision to go outside for components and subassemblies that have traditionally been in-house…there are often attachments that are partially emotional. However, the harsh facts of modern competition make it vital to only expend the precious plant, equipment, and inventory resources on in-house manufacture of components and sub-assemblies (and even final product) where doing so provides a competitive advantage not attainable otherwise. The Momentum Maximizers who maintain the best return on assets from the ongoing business are usually those who have made the best make/buy tradeoff decisions.

Once made, any decision to make something in-house must be carried out with all the attendant implications. If one must do it, then investment in people and equipment must be made to provide world class manufacturing cost and product quality leadership. If one is not prepared to make this kind of commitment, maybe one should consider buying the part from some organization that has shown itself willing to do so.

Inventory Control

Inventory Control in the broadest sense, cuts across the entire organization. As we have seen, many functions, by their action, influence inventory levels. Even in the Utopia of those in this activity...where every item is delivered by the supplier directly to the floor at the precise moment it is needed at that stage of manufacture, there is still inventory in the form of WIP and finished goods to be controlled and minimized. In the "non-ideal" real world there are still stockrooms with log in /log out efficiency and accuracy concerns, security, obsolescence, floor space minimization and a myriad of other factors to balance. (See the discussion on Inventory under "Finance.")

Assembly

One cannot be classified as a "manufacturer" unless one actually puts something together...adds manufacturing labor. One needs at least "Final Assembly" (or perhaps "Final Fill" in a process business) and so on. If an organization receives finished, packaged goods and distributes them, it is a distributor or dealer, not a manufacturer. For the manufacturers of the world, "assembly" in its broad sense is where the production teams efforts come together to create a product. Even steel can be thought of as "assembled" from iron ore, coke, limestone and scrap.

One can visualize Production as a grand "funnel" with Purchasing arranging for the outside procured items, Receiving entering them into the system, Component/sub-assembly Manufacture supplying the flow of in-house made items, Inventory Control overseeing all this material in flow and Production Control orchestrating the process to bring it together at "Final."

Test

Test has also changed over the years. At one time Final Test was the major checkpoint to make sure that the product coming off the end of the line met its specifications. The whole "Quality" program (see discussion under Quality Assurance) has changed that concept radically. The emphasis has shifted to having each stage in the production flow verify the performance of its output (product) against its own specific requirements. Test in this context has become increasingly the responsibility of the operator performing the task, so that the task and its quality verification become one. This constantly improved process facilitates ever-improving first pass yields (at least as long as the product doesn't change).

Shipping

Viewed from the shipping dock, shipping does not appear too much different than it did years ago. The differences are primarily in the shipping arrangements. Momentum maximizing has made a whole science of the process. If a company is too small to do it in-house, specialized consulting firms have sprung up which arrange very attractive rates and service in return for long term commitments on the part of the company. The trucking/freight companies also become more partners than just faceless vendors in this situation.

Process Information Security

Because of the difficulty of monitoring compliance, many firms elect not to patent their core process technology. The security of such proprietary information must therefore be protected by internal controls, rather than in the courts. Frequently such process knowledge (secrets) is wholly or partially stored in the minds of key individual contributors. Process information security, like technical and sales information, must be addressed by the function entrusted. In many industries, the process core competencies are the major differentiating success factors.

VI. CHANGE CREATORS

"There is nothing more difficult to take in hand, more perilous to conduct or more uncertain in its success, than to take the lead in the introduction of a new order of things, because the innovator has for enemies all those who have done well under the old conditions, and lukewarm defenders in those who may do well under the new."

Machiavelli's II Principle   1513 A.D.

Here they come into the picture, the Change Creators. To the Momentum Maximizers, they are as welcome as Jesus was in the seat of Judeo/Roman power in Jerusalem. Jesus Christ, the great "Change Creator," upset the smoothly running arrangements of the High Priests and the Roman bureaucracy of the period, both of the latter outstanding examples of successful "Momentum Maximizers."

In the previous chapters we have seen examples of the diligent effort, on a very broad front, which the Momentum Maximizers have mounted. Each day operations are running more smoothly, more efficiently, more error free. Everyone knows their job and their relationship to others inside and outside the organization. As noted previously, the goal of the Momentum Maximizers is to achieve the best possible results for the longest possible time, with no major change in products, organization or processes.

And now the Change Creators arrive on the scene to disrupt the Momentum Maximizers' nice, smooth-running operation. The goal of the Change Creators is to grow and/or change the direction of the business, in response to the Strategic Plan, by changing the products, markets, processes and even organization, as necessary, to accomplish this end.

The goals of these two groups are not synergistic. Reconciling them requires all the skills and art of senior/general management to maintain things in balance.

In the introduction to the section on Momentum Maximization an example was cited of a situation where there is only Momentum Maximization. There is a flip side situation where there is only Change Creation. That occurs in start-up situations where one or more entrepreneurs, (i.e. Change Creators), get together to nucleate a new business. There is no momentum, (i.e. ongoing business) to maximize.

Once a business like this begins to become successful, and significant portions of sales are momentum, the Change Creator personality frequently does not make the ideal business manager. In most cases, the entrepreneurs are ultimately replaced with individuals with broad spectrum, general management skills.

There have been, throughout history, some notable exceptions. Those rare individuals who can understand and use in others, both Change Creation and Momentum Maximization skills build great companies.

While refining my perception of the roles of Momentum Maximizers and Change Creators, I felt that a similar thought had probably occurred to other students of management theory. Sure enough, Selznick could see, in Pareto's discussion of the roles of the "Foxes" and the "Lions" in geopolitics, an analogy that both of these roles are relevant to business and the need for balance analogous. He points out:

> *"On (Pareto's) discussion of the "circulation of elites" we are offered the hypothesis that the innovator types (the Foxes) are needed to devise new programs and techniques. To be effective, these "Foxes" must be associated with more conservative, forceful elements having strong institutional loyalties and perseverance (the Lions). As the new system or institution gains strength, and has something to defend, the "Foxes" become more expendable; and the "Lions" take over complete control, trimming innovations*

> *to meet the needs of survival. But this in turn may limit adaption to new conditions. The institutional problem is to keep a proper balance of the social types needed at each stage. This theory might well be salvaged and reformulated in more workaday terms for the use in the study of specific institutions, including administrative structures, rather than whole societies…"*

Now we'll get back to the main story. Each of the erstwhile adversaries has distinct advantages. The Momentum Maximizers have a well-established network of "old" relationships and it is the Momentum Maximizers who, from their ongoing operations, provide the cash to fund change. In contrast, since change is frequently accomplished through the use of temporary teams, task forces, etc., the Change Creators are constantly in a mode of feeling their way into new relationships. Since the existence of the Change Creators is justified on "tomorrow's results," they must always contend for funding from today's income.

> *"The universe is change, our life is what our thoughts make it."*
>
> **Marcus Aurelius Antonimus**

The great advantage of the Change Creators is the certainty of change itself. The Momentum Maximizers, in their inner hearts, know that an organization that does not change, as the environment in which it exists changes, is doomed. In this situation, the Momentum Maximizers recognize that they can't avoid change in their tidy world and can only realistically concentrate on "damage control."

In the majority of companies involved in distribution and manufacturing, the Change Creators consist of four main groupings:

1. Marketing (used here in the sense of non-sales marketing activities).
2. Research and Development.

3. Advanced Manufacturing (which has different names in different companies but the same function).
4. Business Development.

They are supported by some elements of "the Score Keepers" and "The Support Suppliers" that are both discussed later.

The emphasis of the Change Creators is on such things as improving time to market, driving to world class manufacturing effectiveness, ROA of the investment in the change process, improvement in market share, penetration of new markets, creating barriers to entry/attack by competitors, changing alliances for improved leverage and/or shared risk/investment, etc.

The following chapters that discuss the various manifestations of Change Creation are not intended to be all-inclusive. It is hoped they will give the reader a flavor of what these folks called Change Creators are all about. Change can be driven from a number of different or even multiple directions, so there is no one starting point. I'll therefore start with what is probably the most visible and talked about - Marketing.

MARKETING

In many companies both sales and non-sales marketing activities are lumped under the title "Marketing" (See "Trojan Horse" discussion). For purposes of this book, Sales (as a Momentum Maximizing activity) is separated and Marketing is used only to refer to those in Marketing specifically involved in the Change Creator role.

Marketing has traditionally had a major role in providing input, recommendations, and proposals to the Strategic Plan. That portion of the job is outside the main focus of this discussion. For our discussion, let us consider that the Strategic Plan, as discussed previously, is already in place.

Therefore, we will group under Marketing the activities associated with creating change. Some of the more typical parts of this Marketing activity are:

1. Market Research
2. Competitor Analysis
3. Product Planning
4. Product Management
5. Trademarks

Market Research

In every organization with whom I have come in contact over the years, the only thing more "painful" to senior management than spending money on the Advance Technology aspect of Research and Development is spending it on Market Research. The Momentum Maximizers, who feel they are the ones who have to earn the money being spent here, present their argument that their Sales people know the market, know the customers and their needs, see the opportunities to expand…so why do we need market research? The market research purists, on the other hand, feel the sales people "can't see the forest for the trees." Obviously, both viewpoints have some validity.

One thing the successful Change Creators learn quickly and their Momentum Maximizer "bankers" soon get the message is…"The most expensive mistake in any product (or process or organizational) development program is incorrect definition of the original requirements." With this in mind, one can afford a great deal of market research, both internal and outside, to avoid even a few such mistakes. Saving money on market research is an example of an expensive "temporary expedient."

"A bad beginning makes a bad ending"

Euripides

Competitor Analysis

Learning from competitors is certainly not a new concept. Aristophanes, Virgil and Ovid all gave that advice in their day.

Competitor analysis in business has grown in stature as a marketing tool and function to the position of a peer activity to customer/market analysis. Marketing people have even "rediscovered" the "Art of War" written 2500 years ago by the Chinese General Sun Tzu and applied his teaching to business competitiveness. Since change usually not only upsets the world of the internal Momentum Maximizers, but also the status quo in the marketplace itself, such change cannot be initiated without an analysis of, and a plan for dealing with, the potential resultant reactions of competitors.

An example of this thinking is some advice that can be called the three "I's." If one wants to take market share away from a competitor without provoking a reaction, one must appear (to the competitor) to be Inconsequential, Irrational or Invincible. Probably old Sun Tzu would agree with this since it is in essence a paraphrase of some of his own quotations.

The ultimate goal of competitor analysis would appear to be plans leading to complete management of the competition so that the competitor does precisely what we wish him to do: permitting us to take away share with minimum reaction, causing the competitor to over invest resources in areas of low interest to us and under invest resources in our target areas. Plans focused on competitors are often part of the Strategic Intent noted previously.

On the other hand, we must be alert to the competition practicing the same tactics on us.

> "The shaft of the arrow had been feathered with one of the eagle's own plumes. We often give our enemies the means of our own destruction"
>
> *Aesop*

(This advice is particularly relevant to sharing ones core competence with a potential competitor)

Product Planning

Product Planning can be viewed as the confluence of several streams of information. Two of these are cited above, Market Research and Competitor Analysis. Other streams are coming from the Research and Development and the Advance Manufacturing parts of Change Creator team discussed below. These provide the technical input to the change plan equation, incorporating current technology trends, long term technology forecasting, new technology impact analysis, technical risk analysis, proprietary protection probability, technical capability assessment, process capability assessment, etc. In addition to these, there are other constraint inputs, such as availability of money and time and fit with the overall Strategic Plan.

Product Planning's role is to pull this together into a proposed plan for a new product or products (or market(s)) complete with financial justification for approval by the appropriate managers. This approval should include the Change Creator management who will implement the plan and the Momentum Maximizer managers whose support and cooperation is vital.

Frequently, the Product Managers (discussed below) also do the Product Planning, but these are still really separate activities and I have chosen to treat them in that manner.

Product Management

"Product Manager" in its broadest sense, is one of the most descriptive business titles ever coined. The job is to shepherd the assigned product from the very start of its life at the approval of the program through the product development phase (as author and guardian of the requirement specification), into product introduction, promotion, market position attainment, financial payback, maturity, and ultimately obsolescence. In an idealized model it is akin to the "Field of Dreams" message "If you build, they will come" except the Product Manager's message is "If you design and manufacture it to meet the requirement specs I have given you, the product will attain the business and commercial success I have predicted."

It is obvious that the Product Manager is traditionally the Marketing representative/advocate of the "Four Horseman of Change Creation."

Trademarks

Trademarks, copyrights and brand names are the marketing form of intellectual property. In our world of explosive exposure to information, it is even more difficult to establish brand and product identity visibility. Well-established company and brand names are major strengths to the holder and as such must be vigorously defended against those who would try to piggyback using the same or too similar appearance, words and names.

RESEARCH AND DEVELOPMENT

The "shock troops" of the Change Creators are the Research and Development people. Even though R&D is only one component of the product development process and even though product development itself is only one aspect of Change Creation, R&D usually has the highest visibility as a Change Creator. R&D expense is the major discretionary expense broken out in company P&L's and annual reports. R&D usually has the most (and the most expensive) people involved in Change Creation. Product development, because its results are manifest, has far more visibility to the outside world than market development (which is often masked) or process development (secret, often unpatented and proprietary).

What then is an R&D organization? The makeup of R&D obviously varies considerably with the industry, the type of product, the mission of the company, etc. Let's start at the "Ivory Tower" end and work our way toward the factory floor.

Research

The "Research" in Research and Development is actually a relatively rare activity in industrial companies. Most pure research is carried out in universities and government (or government sponsored) laboratories. The high cost and long payback time discourage most bottom-line-driven modern industry from "Research." GE's Research Laboratories, which gave us the synthetic industrial diamond, and Bell Labs, which gave us the transistor, are notable (but rare) exceptions.

Another exception is the pharmaceutical companies who must perform or sponsor long, expensive research in their quest for new drugs. This investment in research has been "affordable" to them due to the high mark-ups they were able to obtain in the marketplace for their proprietary products. There is a concern that, if health care reform kills off this golden goose, much of this pharmaceutical research may get "killed" as a by-product.

Since in-house Research is too rich for the average company, but its output is important to the company's future, considerable emphasis must be placed on technology acquisition, discussed later under Business Development.

Applied Research

Applied research/advanced technology is where most companies jump on the bandwagon. This is the arena of technical feasibility where the applicability of a new technology (that is becoming available) to the company's products and business plan is evaluated. Good feasibility studies of new technology that can potentially be employed, and the kind of products that might be developed, is just as critical as the market research on the requirements of the potential customers.

Many advance technology professionals feel that, if even one in ten of the feasibility studies they conduct end up supporting a viable product, the effort is successful. (This "10% yield" thinking is the kind of expectation that can drive the "Score Keepers," in Accounting, crazy, but it's probably not far off the mark on the average).

Just as market research is the most under appreciated part of marketing, the importance of good technical feasibility work is too often the most under-appreciated part of R&D. If one has a good marketing requirement spec based on good market research (as discussed previously) and if all the technology (including process technology) risks and trade-offs is covered by good feasibility studies, then scheduling and implementing the product development effort itself is, not surprisingly, relatively straightforward. We will see however that those two big "ifs" are the reefs on which many otherwise well-conceived product development "ships" founder. And that leads us into the discussion of Development.

Development

Many of the functions (Sales, Production, etc.) discussed previously were made up of individuals with different and complementary skills. In product development this same situation is also the case, and to one of the greatest extents compared to any other part of the organization.

Modern products are so complex that they typically require a wide range of technical skills and technology.

On the skill axis are scientists, engineers, industrial designers, technicians, designers, drafters, model makers, etc. On the technology axis is electrical and electronic engineering, mechanical engineering, physics, computer science, chemistry, microbiology, material science, ergonomics, and a wide, ever expanding list of other technologies, depending on the product.

In this situation, the product development people in R&D, of necessity, began evolving into the team approach many years ago. For each project, a team would be assembled with the required mix of people drawn from the skill and technology capability "pools" within R&D.

There would ordinarily be an R&D Project Leader identified to coordinate the engineering effort. Frequently, the people assigned had not worked together routinely in the past and welding them together to accomplish the task required strong integrative skills. In addition, in order to establish "authority of knowledge" leadership, it was expected that the project leader be knowledgeable in most, if not all, of the skills and technologies involved. Small wonder that project managers who could pull off both these activities were worth their weight in gold.

As far as the product development process itself is concerned, most R&D organizations had evolved some internal project planning and tracking system using phases, or checkpoints, or PERT charts, or Gant charts, or Gates, or what have you, each of which included a map or checklist of what is to be accomplished and when. In the section on Program/Project Management we will see how these arrangements have been broadened and expanded into the battle plan of each specific, coordinated, Change Creator task force.

There are shelves of books on the subject of how to accomplish the R&D task(s) of product development. However, in my experience there is no one universal approach that is best. In any situation there are several that might work and the best choice depends on factors, many of which may be unique to the particular technology, market or company/organization. What is of interest here is Product Development as one of the major manifestations of Change Creation.

During the period preceding the official initiation of a Product Development Program, Marketing, R&D and Advance Manufacturing are often working in a mode of "informed independence"…Marketing working on a number of alternate market research investigations and business alternatives, R&D working on a number of alternate technology feasibilities and Advance Manufacturing exploring new manufacturing process alternatives.

When these three "tribes" come together to sign the Development Authorization for a new product, process or market thrust, it has some of the characteristics of the negotiation of a treaty. In the case of product development for instance, all must reach agreement that a product (or line of products), with characteristics that will permit attainment of a satisfactory business result, can be designed, with an acceptable timetable and resource commitment, utilizing technologies that are (or can be made) available, and manufactured at (or below) the required cost, utilizing manufacturing resources, processes and tooling that is (or can be made) available.

Up to the point of this consensus, Marketing has typically taken on the lead role with the other two in support. Their output is the Requirement Specification. With the signing of the development authorization, leadership is then in the hands of the development people within R&D and remains so at least until the design is verified/qualified through prototypes built to the final design, but not necessarily with the final tooling. R&D's output is a test-proven design sufficiently documented for Manufacturing to produce.

When the design is qualified against the requirements, Advance Manufacturing typically assumes the leadership role through pilot production. Their output is a product or line of products manufacturable at the cost, quality level, inventory level and build rate required. At market introduction, Marketing retakes the lead role. Their output at this point is to obtain the business results promised.

If the program is a market development or process development, as opposed to a product development scenario such as described above, there are similar role responsibilities and sequences.

Adding technical core competence

This is a new and clearer role definition under the R&D umbrella. We have previously defined core competence and have discussed Product Engineering's role in protecting and strengthening those in-house core competencies upon which the competitive success of the current business depend. If a business is to expand into a new area, or even to protect its current markets in a technological shift situation, R&D must be charged with responsibility of obtaining and becoming proficient in, those new technical competencies that are to be built up in-house. Even if a decision is made to utilize a competence obtained via an arrangement with another organization, R&D must still have sufficient in-house familiarity in that field to be able to integrate its use into the product lines.

As the literature on core competence points out, it is very difficult to have the kind of in-depth competence that makes a major competitive difference in a large number of technologies. Just as Marketing must be careful to select those markets (or market segments) to penetrate and/or hold that the company's resources will allow, R&D must select those technologies to penetrate and/or hold that their resources will allow.

Technology Forecasting

Technology forecasting has taken on increased urgency as the pace of technology continues to accelerate (seems like that's getting to be a cliché). Those organizations that can perceive a trend while it is just beginning (and therefore very slight), and have the right combination of perceptiveness, luck and courage, have the potential of building great businesses in very short time frames. We all know the names of those that saw a trend, jumped in ten years ago and are "household names" today. It is critical to every manufacturing organization that its R&D people are trained in, and carry out forecasting of, relevant technologies with the same discipline their marketing associates are applying to market trend forecast. Lest you take this aspect of R&D too lightly, I can cite a very graphic example of the power of technology forecasting and the consequences of ignoring its signals.

In the early 1930s, even though at the time they accounted for less than 0.1% of locomotives being built, some visionaries were touting diesel electric locomotives as an alternate to steam...General Motors gambled on building a plant to make them. General Electric added diesel electrics to its existing line of electric locomotives.

In the same time period, senior executives of the major (at the time) locomotive manufacturers discounted the trend. For instance: "In the future, our railroads will be no more dieselized than they are electrified" - Binkerd of Baldwin Locomotive and "Steam will continue to be the principle railroad motive power" - Dickerman of American Locomotive.

By the mid 1950s, the last steam locomotive had been built and all the traditional locomotive manufacturers, Baldwin, Lima, and American Locomotive, were soon out of the business. GE and GM, the newcomers who read the trend, now dominate the US locomotive market.

One of the really neat things about technology forecasting is that in most instances it appears to follow a logarithmic trend. Extrapolation from very early trend data, when as little as 1% conversion has taken place, can yield amazingly accurate results in many examples.

Sometimes, due to inherent limitations of the new technology, only a portion of a market/application switches over. In a period of about five years, (1973 to 1978) HID lamps took over almost 10% of the commercial and industrial fluorescent lighting fixture business and then plateaued. The fluorescent lamp business was saved (at least temporarily).

Technology acquisition

In the formal contractual sense, this will be discussed in the chapter on "Business Development." However, most technology acquisition in an R&D organization is probably of the informal type. It is not uncommon to hear the plaintive cries of engineering managers buried under mountains of magazines, trip reports, university research, etc. "Please, no more technology …we're drowning in it." The simultaneous explosion of technology and information communication availability pours out information on new technologies at a rate that can overload almost any appraisal system. Really important trends could be missed.

Here is another case where the Core Competence concept can be invaluable. The organization must select (cold-bloodedly) those few technical core competences that it must have in-house to succeed. R&D must use every channel it can to keep abreast of these technologies and those competing technologies that potentially threaten them. The bulk of the rest of the information is therefore "nice to know" but not relevant to the job at hand.

It is important to be technical "cherry pickers" and not "omnivores." Fortunately, the world of computers gives us the ability to search databases by technology, which makes the otherwise overwhelming task manageable. Organizations have sprung up that provide shopping lists of most of the research going on in the free world's universities in a format easy to employ. In short, acquiring technology is usually the easy part. Determining which technologies to acquire is the tough business decision.

Patents

Although Patents are not the exclusive purview of R&D, R&D people obtain most patents. Companies frequently do not patent manufacturing process innovation because it then becomes public knowledge and in the public domain in 17 years. Such matters can be, and are better kept a trade secret. Marketing, on the other hand, is more concerned with the Copywriting and Trademarking side of intellectual property - protecting brands, marks, etc.

Unfortunately the value of patents has fluctuated over the years due to external political factors. In the nineteenth century and the early part of the twentieth, patents were strong and strictly enforceable. Since patents are a form of legal monopoly, they were attacked in the wave of anti-trust furor that began in the 1920s. It became, for a time, very difficult to enforce one's rights particularly if it was perceived as a case of "big business" vs. "the little guy." Disputes were turned over to a highly litigious, and often technologically ignorant court system, and the legitimate rights of patent holders suffered.

The current situation has come back to a more equitable arrangement. Patents can be enforced and special, technology knowledgeable courts have been set up for dispute resolution. This means, that at least in today's climate, patents can provide a significant competitive advantage and every effort should be made to encourage and motivate individuals to obtain this proprietary protection of the core technologies (at a minimum).

Conversely, as the cost of obtaining and maintaining patents (particularly overseas) has steadily risen, and the escalation of technology continued unabated (see NOTE), the task of deciding what to patent has become very difficult. Here again, a well thought out understanding of what the technical core competences of the corporation are and must be, is invaluable as a device for assigning priorities. Priority must then be given first to the rare basic patents and then to "patent fence" patents to surround otherwise unprotectable technology. In overseas patents, the local enforceability and the value of patents in that country as a vehicle for repatriating earnings are considerations.

(NOTE: The pace of technology explosion was brought home to me very personally in 1994. My first patent #2,982,907 issued in 1961. My patent #5,343,368 issued in 1994. The US Patent system was set up over 200 years ago, yet, during this 30-year portion of my professional career, the number of patents has almost doubled.)

One could go on and on about patents, but the bottom line is they can be very important in providing competitive advantage and, although the R&D function may be the custodian, patent decisions are critical decisions of the business and should be held in that focus by the organization.

ADVANCED MANUFACTURING

Perhaps the most difficult flank of the Change Creator Team's assault is that assigned to the Advanced Manufacturing "troops." They have the unpopular task of, all too frequently, disrupting the Production people's smoothly running manufacturing system by introducing new products and new processes. As noted previously, Production includes the veteran Momentum Maximizers of the business, so the task is imposing.

As in the other sections, we'll cover some of the aspects of what I refer to as "Advance Manufacturing." (Although other authors may use different terminology for the function, the role is unchanged) These aspects are representative, not necessarily all-inclusive.

Tooling and Capital Equipment

The design and acquisition of Tooling for new products and processes is an important role of Advanced Manufacturing. Creative industrial engineers are vital members of every Advanced Manufacturing team. Since the cost of this tooling must come out of a capital expense budget, which is in turn frequently capped by overall business considerations, long term and accurate planning and thorough justification is vital. "Claims must be staked out" for the tooling dollars required, right at the point of development project approval or the approval has no meaning.

It is not unusual for the Momentum Maximizers to have urgent needs for some or all of this same annual capital equipment budget to just replace and upgrade, on an evolutionary basis, the worn machinery and aging facilities they have to work with. (They argue that, after all, much of this funding comes, via the depreciation allowance on this very plant and equipment.)

Certain industries find the design of their "tools" (in the broadest sense of the term, including special machine tool, PC board assembly, process machinery, etc.) so vital to their competitive success, that they make the design and manufacture of such items a core competency and treat it as such. In such situations, this aspect of Advance Manufacturing is elevated to a major business strategic consideration.

In the majority of cases however, the non-repetitiveness of the type of tools and/or the expense of maintaining a core competence compared to other resource demands, dictate that Advance Manufacturing more often farm out the design and manufacture of tools to outside organizations who specialize in the skill required. As in the case of other farmed out competencies, Advance Manufacturing must have the in-house skill to control and monitor these suppliers.

Process Development

Process Development may occur as a part of a new product development or may be a radical change in the way an existing product or products is made available with no new product involved. (Long-range, manufacturing process development responsibility is discussed below under Forecasting). Bringing a product/process in-house, or farming out a former process in-house, are examples of major change. The whole thrust to being "global" has added a new dimension. Global sourcing, co-manufacture, internationally substitutable sub-assemblies are really all process development.

Prototyping

Another of the assignments, within the product development team, which ordinarily falls to the Advance Manufacturing members, is arranging for the procurement of prototypes. Ever-tightening scrutiny of R&D expense has led to the demise of the "model shop." Such operations were found not to be cost effective, with one factor being the high cost of maintaining a "readiness to serve" with typically cyclical demand, another being the cost of keeping these facilities up to date with all the newest manufacturing methods and materials, and a third (less obvious) one being the lack of management skills and training among R&D people in running what is in essence, a small manufacturing activity.

The slack has typically been picked up by Advance Manufacturing, who is expected, by combinations of tool room time, breaking into production flow, technicians and outside sourcing, to provide the prototypes that R&D and Marketing need.

Procurement

Frequently new product development and new process development require establishing a relationship with a new vendor/supplier/partner. For this reason most Advance Manufacturing operations include purchasing/procurement specialists. These new relationships require almost a two-way qualification process. Unilateral vendor qualification is becoming passé as really good suppliers find they can't afford to waste their precious competency on an industrial customer that hasn't "got its act together" and/or doesn't afford an attractive return potential. Mutually qualifying each other for a long-term relationship related to a new product or process requires special skills in Advanced Manufacturing procurement.

Process Development Forecasting

Process technology forecasting and planning is just as important as the product related technology forecasting alluded to previously. We are familiar with the old experience curves that showed the opportunity for a 20% reduction in real cost with every doubling of cumulative volume. This phenomenon can be used in the support of the contention that a market leader who reinvests cannot be caught unless there is a paradigm shift in the basic process technology that upsets the basic assumptions of the experience curve.

The market leader must, therefore, be alert and tracking all process technology that might conceivably upset the cost/quality/manufacturability of its products. Conversely, those companies with smaller shares of the market must be looking diligently for any change in process technology that would allow them to overcome the cost advantage of the leader, who they hope is over committed to existing technology. Once again, core competence concepts can help the Advance Manufacturing process gurus identify which process technologies are critical to the organization's competitive advantage and focus there.

PROGRAM/PROJECT MANAGEMENT

When a multifunctional team is assembled to carry out a specific project, a project leader is normally assigned/selected to spearhead the program. Depending on the particular corporate culture, this role may range all the way from a strong, dominant boss personality, through committee chairman consensus facilitator type, to (occasionally) more of an administrator of a truly self-directed team. In any case, the individual has typically proven himself or herself in similar leadership roles in one of the Change Creator sub-groups. In my experience, only rarely is a Momentum Maximizer background individual selected.

This individual must provide beginning-to-end continuity. As the relative importance of different functions change throughout the course of the project, marketing, R&D and advance manufacturing personnel assigned will normally change over the life of the project. I feel that it is vitally important to senior management and to the other parts of the organization that need visibility of the progress of the activity, that the project/program leader not be changed during the task if at all possible.

We reviewed earlier the R&D Project Leader role, the individual who directs the efforts of all the R&D personnel assigned to the project. This role continues even in the era of the overall Program/Project Manager. The skill sets of the two jobs are quite different.

The ideal Program/Project Manager would be:

A. An excellent organizer and administrator.

B. An excellent integrator of the diverse skill sets and personalities assigned (including people skills).

C. An excellent communicator and salesman in presenting the team to the rest of the organization.

D. An excellent measurer and controller of resources and results.

E. Highly self-motivated, highly focused.

F. Sensitive to the politics in the larger organization within which the team must function.

G. Skilled in inducing the cooperation of the key Momentum Maximizer leaders and personnel being impacted.

H. Most of all, understanding of the overall mission, the particular strategic plan and the role of the project within that plan.

One can see that this is an imposing list of capabilities. In my view, developing people with these kinds of skills is something like raising exotic plants in a hothouse. They must be nurtured (mentored) by experienced senior executives. They must be fed (rewarded/recognized for accomplishment). They must not be improperly exposed to the elements (criticized for a disappointing outcome which occurred for reasons beyond their control) when they did their task well. In all the organizations to whom I've been exposed in my business life, I have never seen these three management development guidelines followed to the extent I feel is required to grow such capabilities, yet the existence of such capability could be a real "core competence" for the organization.

Program/Project Managers today have available the most sophisticated planning and control systems one could envision, mountains of information instantly available via their computer terminals and wide-ranging communications capability. Newer management thinking on team empowerment gives better control of the team's destiny by the team. The very "melting pot" mentality of Americans perhaps fits the multifunctional team approach better than any other nation.

It is no accident that Japanese businessmen spend so much time achieving "Ringi" (complete agreement and consensus) before they embark on a project. Their culture perhaps does not let them easily adapt to the flexible, constantly readjusting style that modern American Change Creator Teams can and do employ. On the other side of the globe, in many of the industrialized states of Europe, the Momentum

Maximizers have become so entrenched that the Change Creators have a rougher time in carrying out their vital role in keeping their industries healthy in changing conditions.

American industry (and the nation itself for that matter) has one of the best change creation capabilities of any developed nation on earth. Where we have had business failures, it has tended to be more in the "Mission," "Intent" and "Strategic Planning" areas.

BUSINESS DEVELOPMENT

The realities of global competition have done what the NAM, or any of its members, was never able to accomplish…force the U.S. government to put monopoly and anti-trust concerns into a more sensible perspective. With overseas companies (and even their governments) free to make alliances and work together for mutual self-interest, American companies were being penalized at the very time when the escalation and cost of technology were making it almost prohibitive to "go it alone" on all fronts. Thankfully, that situation is now changing. Partially as a result of that attitudinal change, one function has received new status as a major aspect of Change Creation - the Business Development professional. Another factor that has also reinforced the new position of Business Development among the Change Creators is the focus on such considerations as Intent, Strategic Planning, Competencies, etc.

As most well run existing businesses have zeroed in on whom they were and where they were headed, the number of true "orphan" businesses in their current portfolio became more highly visible. The resulting decisions to spin off have required Corporate Development capability in both the spinner and the receiver. Conversely, the identification of "holes" in the armamentaria of competencies needed, which cannot economically (in time or money) be developed in-house, often requires Corporate Development skills in acquiring these competencies from the outside.

This "Fourth Horseman" of the Change Creator Cavalry (The others being Market Development, Product Development and Process Development) is in the lead for those aspects of the Strategic Plan that call for achieving portions of the Strategic Intent via acquisitions, divestitures and major partnerships.

There are many types of acquisitions/divestures, so I'll just touch on three of the major types. Before launching into that discussion, I'll share the great "secret" of successful acquisition negotiation. Successful acquisitions are those where one plus one adds up to more than two, i.e., because of a better match, the business/ product/ technology is worth more to the acquirer than to the divestor. Only in that circumstance is there enough benefit to both parties to provide the incentive to do it.

Acquisition of a business

The type of acquisition that gets the most publicity, even though it is the fewest in number, is the acquisition of an entire business. This sort of thing naturally involves an enormous commitment of resources on the part of both parties (and their expensive legal and financial associates) to reach the agreement and an even greater and more sustained commitment to make it work afterward. There are plenty of books and experts on the due diligence process and on contract terms - that part just takes the time of capable people and money.

The failures I've seen over the years seldom related to just a technical or financial mistake in these areas. The failures more often involve a breakdown in that area of "soft technology" called business culture (and the resultant opportunity for cultural mismatch therein). It's bad enough with big company versus small company culture, or privately owned versus public companies, where both are in the U.S. The drive to be global has added the complexity of ethnic and language cultural differences. To me, this whole area of identifying acquisitions (and spin offs) with reasonable probability of cultural success and business success (that's an "and," not an "or"), and then making it happen, is the greatest challenge to Business Development via business acquisition/divesture.

Product line acquisition

Acquisition of product lines and technology occurs far more frequently, but with less fanfare. Product lines are often identified as "orphans" by their owners, but may fill in a gap for a potential acquirer. Not only can product line acquisition be less expensive than internal development, but it also permits the simultaneous "purchase" of a market share position without having to "take it away" from someone in the marketplace. (Old General Sun Tzu, alluded to in the section on Marketing, was also an advocate of not fighting if you can achieve your goal via negotiation.)

Acquiring a product line typically involves relocating it to your own facilities once the function of Corporate Development has negotiated the deal. At this point, the task of relocation is assigned to a multifunctional team usually headed up by the best Advanced Manufacturing project leader, who must be prepared to spend a lot of time away from home working with potentially and possibly uncooperative, divestor personnel.

Acquisition of technology

Technology acquisition is probably the most common type of acquisition. Here the trick is to convince another organization that possesses a technology that your organization needs for its future success, to turn over access on business terms that are a "good deal" for both parties (no small task in the really "hot" technologies). We are talking here primarily about technologies that are being acquired to be brought in-house. As noted in the discussion on Procurement, technology access is also achieved in products being supplied by a supplier/partner, but these situations can often be handled at the purchasing operations level.

This leads naturally into the subject of Partnerships.

Partnerships

This has proven to be the most difficult section for me to write. I don't know if that is because I feel so strongly about it that I am afraid of not being convincing enough or that I feel the power of this technique is so obvious that it needed no justification. However, as with many great concepts, there is also a "dark side" and some gray regions as well. So I guess there is no way of avoiding it, we really must address partnerships in a relationship sense not the legal organization sense.

We have seen the importance of mission, intent and strategy. We have covered the importance of core competencies. If all of these mesh for an organization, based on internal planning and capabilities, then there is no driving need to seek partnerships. This is not to say that the organization might not be sought out as a partner by another, not so self sufficient, organization.

It is only when the plans of a company require major competencies (critical success factors) that the organization does not possess, that partnerships may be considered. Typically, before seeking such a relationship, the organization must first come to the conclusion that it would not be effective, either in time or money, to acquire the competency from outside (see acquisition discussion) or develop it internally.

As in the case of acquisitions, the best partnerships are those where one plus one is more than two. One organization brings to the relationship its set of competencies for addressing the target opportunity. The partner organization brings such a complimentary set of competencies to the table that, together, the partnership can gain a level of success in an area that neither could have achieved on their own. Sounds straightforward, doesn't it? Well, it isn't at all straightforward.

Let us assume two previously autonomous businesses, which have previously enjoyed freedom to act on their own. They find they share a mutual goal. Further, let us assume that, between them, they possess all the main competencies required to achieve that goal. They decide to discuss a partnership relationship. What might be some of the questions that should be asked? Here are a few:

Question #1 - Is the chemistry excellent between the principals of the two organizations? Fifteen years ago, I might not have put this as question #1. However, during those intervening years, I have had the opportunity to serve in a consulting and/or corporate development role, for a number of successful, family-owned and managed corporations. Over a period of years, I brought to the principals of these businesses a number of, what looked to me, like good deals.

I learned from these owners/senior management that, no matter how good the deal looks like on paper, if they personally didn't feel completely comfortable with the prospective partner's management people, there was no sense going further. The lesson is that all the detailed contract language I could write was no substitute for good people chemistry right at the start. Often these individuals made it a point to get together in an informal, away from the office setting, with the prospective counterparts. If that went okay, then we could start to do serious negotiation.

Question #2 - Will the same principals be in place when the partnership is implemented? This is when partnerships become more difficult if one (or both) of the businesses are part of a large public corporation.

As all of us who have been in business for a number of years have experienced, in that circumstance the players can change overnight and with them may go the chemistry and trust upon which the partnership was based.

On the other hand, most large corporations are understandably reluctant to give "veto power" on internal personnel changes to a partner organization. However, in some instances that is what a really close, tight partnership may require. In these cases, unwillingness to meet the need for continuity of top level, what I would call "business friendships," between the parties can be a deal breaker. From this viewpoint, it is easier for two privately held businesses to make a long-term commitment to each other.

Question #3 - Are the two organizations culturally compatible? All the factors, previously cited in this area under acquisitions, apply doubly here. In this venue, the ideal match would be two privately held companies, of about the same size and age, from the same geographical area of the USA and either both based in a small town or both big city based. At the other end of the spectrum, the most difficult match is a modest size, family-owned, small town based company in one country and a division of a large public company based in a different country with different language, customs, business practices, etc. Most situations lie somewhere in between these extremes. If objective analysis says the cultures are so incompatible that the partnership will take decades to really work, most U.S. businesses would back off. It should be noted that, in the Orient, a relationship that takes decades to build is not viewed as unusual…. another cultural difference.

Question #4 - Are the two organizations of similar size and power?

> *"There are no compacts between lions and men and wolves and lambs have no compact."*
>
> Homer

In general, the relationship large automobile companies have with their typically smaller parts suppliers is not a true partnership. One party is so powerful that they control the other's destiny almost completely. I recall an instance where someone I knew worked for a fairly good size supplier to one of the big three. When the supplier appeared to be in danger of missing a commitment, the auto company just sent in their own team to take over and run the operation. The suppliers' own management were, in essence, pushed aside for the duration of the crisis.

In a similar vein, the relationship major companies in Japan have with their cottage industry suppliers are not really partnerships.

One can have a partnership between a modest size company and a similar size, reasonably autonomous division of a large corporation. This obviously also applies to partnerships between such autonomous divisions of two different companies.

Question #5 - Will both parties have in place dedicated individuals whose primary job is to represent (with full authority) their organization in the relationship and co-manage the partnership? Just like machinery, partnerships need continual preventive maintenance. I have heard of organizations going so far as to "exchange hostages" where the company's representative is actually resident at the partner's facility.

Question #6 - Are both parties willing to surrender some degree of complete freedom to control their business? Partnership often requires some degree of "yoking" in the area of the common goal. I saw a deal that passed all the other tests with flying colors fall apart when, at almost the last minute, one of the owners couldn't bring himself to surrender some of his previous complete autonomy. This is an area where family-owned businesses may have more problems than divisions of public companies.

Question #7 - Is there a method, built into the agreement, to adjust the terms if some change in the technology, market, political climate, etc. makes the deal significantly less advantageous to one party? A partnership must, on an ongoing basis, be a good deal for both parties. The up front intent, and the contract language that formalizes it, must be flexible enough to permit changes and adjustments to keep it a fair balance of benefit.

Question #8 - Is there a mechanism set up to terminate the partnership if circumstances change (beyond any adjustment range)? Termination is difficult enough without waiting until it's about to happen to work on the mechanics. Both parties should agree to the termination arrangement in the original agreement, when everyone is hopefully optimistic and objective.

I could go on and on with the questions, but I think the reader can catch the flavor with just these. There are whole books on all the details involved in performing due diligence studies on potential acquisitions.

Organizational Development

One cannot begin a discussion of Organizational Development without at least acknowledging the historic perspective. There is an excellent quotation on the subject:

> *"We trained hard, but it seemed that every time we were beginning to form up into teams, we would be reorganized. I was to learn later in life that we tend to meet any new situation by reorganizing, and a wonderful method it can be for creating the illusion of progress, while producing confusion, inefficiency and demoralization."*

This sounds like a moan of despair from last week's latest "corporate reengineering," but in fact, it is a quote from the 66 A.D. writings of Gaius Petronius, the 1st century Roman Prefect of Egypt. (So much for thinking organizational development and its abuses are modern phenomenon).

Just as markets, technology and processes are always changing, requiring the company that is to be successful to anticipate and move to capitalize on change, so also are organizational concepts. Today it is hard for those of us in the developed nations to imagine what it was like to operate in the authoritarian/ "industrial slave" mode of the early industrial revolution. We seldom stop to think that it will be just as difficult for people 100 years from now, to visualize what it was like to operate in the organization concepts of the year 2001. It is just as key to future success to anticipate the direction of organizational development as any other trend, and take action upon that vision.

Certainly the advent of the information/communication/computer/robot era offers a whole new set of conditions that are bound to reshape organizations. It may be that the whole culture of physically coming together to a central location to go "to work" will disappear. Will we be better decentralized? How can this be organized? How will we integrate robots and artificial intelligence into human organizations?

These may sound like far out questions but it is important to think through and have a vision. Organizational change that can be evolved deliberately against a long-range plan has the best chance of being accomplished with minimum "confusion, inefficiency and demoralization."

It is interesting to consider that, almost alone in human activities, organizations are usually designed by those who will operate within them. Boat designers/builders don't sail the ships. Airplane designers/builders don't fly the planes. Machinery designers/builders don't run the machines...and so on. The skills or mind set required to design are not necessarily the same skill set needed to operate. It may be that better results can be achieved, if individuals, skilled at designing an organization that is best structured to carry out the mission, set it up and others were put in to operate/manage. (I know that the most successful organizational-set-up I ever performed was one in which I was not personally going to have an operational role once it was set up. I could be completely objective.)

One road to ruin is to let the salesmen design the commission plan. Enron showed another road to ruin in which the executives apparently designed a structure that rewarded them for actions that damaged the business. Maybe it's time to consider utilizing professional designers of organization to put in place the structure for the professional managers to then function within.

Probably far too often, changing the organization may be only treating the symptom rather than the deeper-seated cause. Unfortunately there are many in Organization Development (and I have probably been among them at times) who appear to be saying, to paraphrase Will Rogers, "I never met an organization I didn't like…. to change."

THREE TROJAN HORSES

With the Momentum Maximizers striving to protect the base business and wring the most from current markets, products and processes, and the Change Creators simultaneously endeavoring to change any and all of these, and thereby upset the Momentum Maximizer's smoothly running operation, how can businesses continue to function? The solution that has evolved retains the structure of the old functional organization (at least on the surface) to provide the Change Creators with "Trojan Horses" to get inside the Momentum Maximizers "fortress."

We find the Change Creator Marketing Team typically reports to the same senior Marketing Executive (now in the broad sense of the term) as the Momentum Maximizer's Sales Team. They both can think of themselves as part of one "tribe." Similarly, the Change Creator's R&D group reports to the same Technology Executive as the Momentum Maximizer's Product Engineering and another "tribe" is in place. Finally, the Change Creator's Advanced Manufacturing is usually under the same Manufacturing Executive's wing as the Momentum

Maximizer's Production people-both part of the "Manufacturing Tribe."

To a great degree, it is this use of the ancient tribal instincts of the human race that facilitates the work of the Change Creators. Each of the old functional tribes feels that "it is our own people who are involved in this change and they understand our problems and will be careful in tampering with our smoothly running operation."

"Man is a social animal."

Spinoza

The old functions of Marketing, Engineering and Manufacturing have therefore, to some degree, provided the "Trojan Horses" to enable the Change Creators to work from inside and the Momentum Maximizers to accept them. This accommodation does place a major responsibility on these three senior functional managers to balance the two forces at work within their organizations to achieve the best long-term result.

VII. SCORE KEEPERS

"When you can measure what you are speaking about, and express it in numbers, you know something about it; but when you cannot measure it, when you cannot express it in numbers, your knowledge is of a meager and unsatisfactory kind…"

Lord Kelvin

The role of the Score Keepers is a vital one. They provide the information and tools to help the Momentum Maximizers, the Change Creators and their Support Suppliers measure their progress against their goals and objectives so they can take appropriate action. They provide senior management with the information they require to make their business decisions and they may provide data to other stakeholders such as stockholders, government agencies, etc.

There are at least three clearly identified Score Keeper roles and so we'll start first with Accounting.

ACCOUNTING

The Encyclopedia Britannica defines accounting as "the art of recording, classifying, and summarizing transactions of an enterprise and interpreting the results thereof." Although the Babylonians, Greeks and Romans used contracts and kept farm accounts, accounting as a general business tool dates more to the 14th century when double entry bookkeeping was introduced first in Genoa, and then Florence, next in the Italian States, and soon thereafter, in the Hanseatic League. Two important, but possibly under-appreciated inventions in accounting made a major difference in the usefulness of the tool.

The first was the concept of converting all assets and liabilities into a common method of measurement - their currency equivalent. Only by this breakthrough could one "balance" such different things as buildings, bushels of grain due, oxen, licenses, etc., on a double entry set of books.

The other, equally important concept, was that of viewing an organization as a separate "entity" in itself, separate and distinct from the government officials, church hierarchy, individuals, etc., who created it.

I trace the history to make the point that the role of the accountant has always been (and in my mind it is important that this role remain clear) to be a Score Keeper. The Senior Management and their Momentum Maximizers and Change Creators simply cannot do their job without timely, relevant, concise, objective, quality data to allow them to make their management decisions. It is important, however, to not get the two "d's" confused. The accountant provides data, not decisions; line management cannot escape that responsibility.

If the accountants were considered like a monastic order, surely the abbot would be the Comptroller (Controller). This individual has the overall primary responsibility to see to it: that the organization receives accurate, timely and relevant business reports; that records are maintained; that the physical assets are accounted for; that liabilities are kept visible; that income and other tax information is prepared; that budgets are prepared; etc.

Further, the Comptroller is frequently charged with interpreting financial reports and similar business statistics to make sure that all the interested parties "know the score" and understand its implications. For instance, in most companies, the controller and the accountants are also responsible for providing information to the third party stakeholders such as banks, stockholders, governments, etc.

(See also the portion of the Comptrollers job that is considered "Support.")

QUALITY ASSURANCE

The second group of Scorekeepers is the Quality Assurance people. Unlike the Accountants, these people are relative newcomers to major status in the operations of business. There have been inspectors at least as far back as the pyramids, but as we move into the 21st century, that kind of Quality Assurance role is rapidly disappearing in modern American industry. The change is relatively recent. Even references as late as the 1975 edition of the Encyclopedia Britannica defined Quality Control as:

> *"assurance of the conformity of manufactured products to estab-lished specifications by systematic observation and regulation of starting materials, workmanship, or other influences."*

The change in the status and practice of Quality Assurance sprang, to a great extent, from the "rediscovery of quality" in the 1970s and 1980s. Quality as a major focus in manufacturing had been "demoted" many years before when the industrial revolution overran and crushed the old craft and guild systems along with their emphasis on pride of workmanship.

Certainly, part of the credit for the rebirth of quality goes to the gurus like Deming. One wonders, however, if the escalation would have been as rapid, had not the Japanese manufacturers seized upon quality as their change creating "new development" (their paradigm shift) to penetrate the American market from which they previously had been largely excluded.

The new Quality Assurance focuses on the individual (or teams of individuals) taking responsibility for their own work (shades of the craft system) with the Quality Assurance organizations role being to provide the training, measurements and tools to enable the individual worker to measure quality of output. In the ideal situation, one would have an "inspectorless" factory. Even the time honored practice of incoming inspection can vanish with the advent of qualified supplier partners whose quality is such that their components can be delivered directly to production.

The last few decades have seen the explosion of the service industry. Quality Assurance is just as relevant to that industry (an application not even anticipated by the cited Encyclopedia definition 20 years previous).

As in the case of Accounting, it is important that the Quality Assurance personnel's role is kept as pure as possible to Score Keeping. There is a natural temptation, in smaller organizations, to have the Q/A people also perform some synergistic operational jobs such as handling returns and/or repair in addition to their Score Keeping. I feel this is a mistake in any reasonable size organization since it inhibits their ability to be objective scorekeepers. (You don't see referees shooting foul shots!)

OUTSIDE REGULATORY (AND OTHER) BODIES

The number of Federal regulatory agencies has grown very rapidly since 1900 and the state and local governments have paralleled the growth with their own agencies. At the beginning of the century, there were only five federal regulatory agencies and by the year 2000 there were over sixty. Many of these federal and local agencies impact the way business is conducted today. In addition, there are many non-government outside Score Keepers (i.e., credit bureaus, better business organizations, consumer protection groups, and a host of other (primarily non-profit) special interest and watchdog groups).

All of these outsiders are keeping score on the business. If anything, these organizations are tougher for the Change Creators to deal with, since they more often come into play when something is, or is planning to be, changed.

VIII. SUPPORT SUPPLIERS

Somehow in our culture, the concept of being a support supplier (like the allied concept of being a "servant") has taken on a negative aspect. The soldier "at the front" or "hitting the beach" is idealized more than those in the supporting supply line that provide the means to get him there, keep him there and without whom he will surely fail. The fact is, both are interdependent and vital. Many military historians believe that the defeat of the Luftwaffe in the battle for Britain was at least partially attributable to the Luftwaffe's lack of a logistics system (for repairs and spares).

The simple fact is that the senior management, the Momentum Maximizers and the Change Creators cannot carry out their roles without the services provided by the Support Suppliers. It is also a fact however, that the results and efficiency of the efforts of the Support Suppliers themselves are harder to measure than those of the people for whom they provide support. As a result, support organizations either "run to fat" or are frequently perceived as doing so by the operations people. Conversely, it is the "operations" people who scream the loudest when support isn't responsive.

It is a tough, important management call to determine and put in place the level of support staffing and expense required, and an equally tough, important management call to not let it exceed or fall below that level.

HUMAN RESOURCES

In my experience, of all the Support Suppliers, the one that appears embroiled in the most controversy is Human Resources. This is understandable since this function deals exclusively with the most subjective and difficult to predict and control aspect of the organization - the human beings that make it up.

Since the function has so many aspects, they are grouped into four classes: "Helping them Come," "Helping them Stay," "Helping them Grow" and "Helping them Leave."

"Helping Them Come"

This is probably the area where it is easiest to obtain job gratification for the Human Resource professional. It includes recruiting, verifying qualifications, selling the opportunity to the prospective employee, interviewing, arranging physicals and other testing, obtaining acceptance of all the contractual aspects (confidentiality agreements, patent agreements, tax forms, etc., providing proof of employment (badges, etc.), arranging for orientation, and so on.

This activity is clearly all upbeat and positive. It is important, however, in the midst of all this euphoria, to lay the groundwork for all the other aspects of future contact of the employee with Human Resources. This is an aspect of the orientation process that is easy to overlook, but which, if done properly, can allow the employee to receive future involvement with Human Resources with a better degree of understanding.

"Helping Them Stay"

This is the part of the job that traditionally occupies most of the time in HR. It starts out with a few reasonably objective tasks but "gets personal" pretty quickly. One of these tasks, which may appear completely objective, is also one of the more difficult and turns out to be somewhat subjective. That task is position evaluation, the process of determining initially, and verifying constantly, the compensation range appropriate and competitive for each position in the organization.

For most positions, there is peer comparison data available for a guideline, but the value of many of the management and professional positions are also a function of how they relate to the current and future strategies of the company. For instance, an engineering position intended to supplement one of the company's key core competencies is obviously worth offering more for, to attract the right individual, than some national engineering average salary curves might indicate.

Some major companies have attempted to address the problem by moving toward fewer "steps" in the grade ladder but with much broader salary/compensation ranges at each step. This gives the individual manager more flexibility in attracting and holding people with widely different levels of training, experience and potential. This concept does, however, place a demand for a greater level of sophistication on the part of lower and middle level managers. This aspect worries Human Resource professionals, in particular in the areas of equal opportunity for women and minorities in that it makes such compliance harder to monitor.

Another set of considerations is that of balancing being externally competitive when recruiting, but still maintaining equity with the compensation of existing employees with similar skills. This balancing act can be particularly difficult in times when industry wide skill shortages cause subsequent rapidly rising, starting salary offers.

Succession Planning

Another important and rewarding job for the HR professional is to coordinate succession planning for all the planned key roles for the future. It is a necessary activity for a healthy, growing company, but one that must be carried out with great concern for confidentiality and privacy. All the managers and key individual contributors must be involved in providing input but the resultant action plan must be essentially invisible to avoid "crown princes (or princesses)" on one hand, and the loss or demoralization of important, but not as promotable personnel on the other.

Salary and Benefit Administration

Salary administration involves providing guidelines to the client functions on the range of merit increases, and the ideal target average for the next salary period. Once again, peer comparisons are available, but management and professional people tend to compare their progress nationally, whereas office workers and factory employees are more apt to look at the local economy. Special attention must be given to the satisfaction of the repositories of the core competences of the corporation. Human Resources also has the unenviable task of watching for any signs of "socialistic salary administration," i.e., the tendency of some supervisors to "take the easy way" and give everyone the same increase, independent of contribution and competitive value.

In today's world, an even tougher task than salary administration is benefit administration. We have lived to see the day when the health insurance costs of the workers involved exceed, on a per car basis, the cost of the steel used in the construction of the automobile. All these non-salary costs, and particularly medical care, have become such a major cost factor that it has distorted the economics of hiring practices. The problem is so acute and universal that almost all organizations, including churches and charities, find it more economic to work their employees overtime rather than take on the incremental benefit hit that goes with hiring additional employees.

It is probably unlikely, in my view, that Congress is going to find a way to quickly change the situation. If they could, the immediate result would be that the workweek would shorten and unemployment shrinks further. In the meantime, Human Resources is doomed to fight a "rear guard action" in trying to limit the negative impact of health care costs on the operations of the business.

Good News - Bad News

Since this rear guard action often involves perceived take aways, this is about as good a place as any to insert two relevant quotes from Machiavelli.

> *"For injuries ought to be done all at one time, so that, being tasted less, they offend less; benefits ought to be given little by little, so that the flavor of them last longer."*

and

> *"...princes (read senior management) ought to leave matters of reproach to the management of others, and to keep those of grace in their own hands."*

This sounds like excellent advice and it relates to one of the many ways that Human Resources supports Senior Management. If there is going to be bad news, i.e., "taking away" in the form of either salaries, benefits, cutbacks, etc., it is best if Human Resources, together with non-senior management, deliver it. Furthermore, it is better to do it all at once, even at the risk of going too far (and having to later on back off), than to do it by dribs and drabs so that everyone sits around "on pins and needles" waiting for "the other shoe to drop."

The advice also implies that Senior Management should be perceived as the giver of positive, attractive things like Christmas bonuses, patent awards, service awards, performance awards, etc. (Incidentally, it sounds like, if Machiavelli were running the show, he'd probably use monthly or quarterly bonuses rather than one at year's end.)

Machiavelli was certainly a perceptive man. It has constantly amazed me, in all my years in industry, how anxious employees are to blame Human Resources for bad news even though HR was usually only carrying out the directions of the Senior Management. Conversely, it seems that employees want to think well of, and have faith in, the Senior Management's judgment and concern for them and don't want to have to associate them with bad news or bad judgment.

Another job of HR has that doesn't win popularity poles, is laying down the guidelines for employee-employee and employee-supervisor relationships. This covers the gamut from attendance, dress code, harassment, discrimination, disciplinary actions and smoking policy to performance appraisals, promotion criteria, and personal development.

Still another difficult task that falls to HR is dealing with third party employee representatives (e.g., unions) or being charged with pro-employee programs aimed at assuring the employees that such third party involvement is unnecessary and not in the employee's interest. Both of these are formidable tasks and require focused, every day attention in order to conserve the operations people.

"Helping Them Grow"

Amidst all these potentially polarizing tasks, HR is expected to carry out two activities that require that the employee have faith in the HR people as being there to help them. The first of these is training in those areas that cut across the company's functional lines. This might include training of new managers in management techniques and finance, company wide quality training (that may span years), communication skills training, etc. Since many of these activities may include taking time outside of normal working hours, and the time spent during working hours is normally not offset by any reduction in on-the-job performance requirement, they represent inducing the employee to make an extra commitment.

This is the sort of commitment that, if obtained, can have the subtle effect of reinforcing employee loyalty and allegiance to the company. This tendency is noted by Machiavelli who observed:

"For it the nature of man to be bound by the benefits they confer as much as by those they receive."

I recall an occasion where things were not going well for a particular division of a major corporation and the management asked everyone, including themselves, to come in and work one week without pay to allow the division to make the year. There was enough shared commitment among the people that they did just that and, in doing so, drew closer together than they had ever been before that pact. I have seen many times when such a challenge can be very motivating to an entire group or team. (In the particular organization cited above, that sense of bond and common purpose was destroyed a few years later when there was a "boom" (way over plan) year with no reciprocal extra weeks' pay for those who had participated in meeting the previous challenge. Something was lost and I don't believe it was ever regained.

Counseling

To return to the HR discussion, the other activity requiring the trust and cooperation of the employee is in counseling. It is important that the employee be provided every possible channel for problem resolution. The first line of contact should normally be the employee's immediate supervisor, but if that individual cannot resolve it (or is perhaps part of the problem) then HR is expected to stand ready to provide this assistance.

These two roles, compared to those that preceded, are clearly difficult to rationalize. If HR must "wear the black hat" and be perceived as the "taker away" to allow senior management the "white hat," how can the employee see HR as his coach, confidant and friend ("on their side") in the latter roles?

I have sometimes thought that maybe the present HR ought to be broken into two parts to allow the employees to at least rationalize the dichotomy. Perhaps put the training, counseling, personal development, pro-employee programs etc., using the old Employee Relations title together with some other, non-threatening support function like Community Relations (below). Then one could let the balance of HR function in a less ambivalent manner.

"Helping Them Leave"

> *"They're terribly fond of beheading people here. The great wonder is that there's anyone left alive."*
>
> **Lewis Carroll's "Alice in Wonderland"**

In recent years, this part of HR activity has had much more visibility. As companies struggle to succeed in the new global competitive environment some have turned to "downsizing" or "reengineering the organization" (or similar euphemisms) to reduce costs and improve productivity. The net result of these approaches has been to place a major burden on HR to facilitate the subsequent reductions, retraining, or reassignment of personnel. Termination (or "out placement"), retraining, and early retirement packages are major activities requiring specialized skills.

Even the activities and changes that are normal byproducts of these events escalate. These extra retirees coupled with new accounting rules have made, and are making, pension administration even more difficult. Rising health care costs have driven up the costs of retiree health benefits far above the level anticipated a few years ago.

Human Resource Summary

I think that the reader can see that Human Resources, even though cast as a "support" function, impact all aspects of the operation. Its management and its performance are vital to the success of all its "client" operations activities and the company.

FINANCE

The other major "player" in the Support Suppliers is Finance. Although Accounting is normally administratively under "Finance," its function is really primarily "Scorekeeping" and has been covered in that section. All of the other sub functions, that typically fall under Finance, in a manufacturing concern, are really support to the operating units.

Even as the traditional financial role has become more complex and interwoven to a greater degree into the very fabric of the enterprise, Finance has also taken a stronger role in "advising and counseling" in the strategic planning process itself. In spite of these changes, however, Finance in manufacturing companies, is still not considered an "operational" role.

Just as HR arranges for all the human resources services, my view of Finance is as the arranger for all the non-people resources. Further, Finance establishes and maintains internal controls to protect assets, cash in excess of operational needs, receivables, inventories, etc. Since, as noted in the discussion on accounting, non-people resources get measured and are acquired and disposed of in currency and currency equivalents, Finance must seamlessly manage the flow of cash so all that the operational parts of the organization can function.

Cash comes in primarily from the sales of goods and services, from license fees, from sale of stock and from borrowings from the bank.

Cash is then used to meet payroll expense, pay suppliers for goods and services purchased, pay for capital investments in plant and equipment, pay license fees, pay taxes, pay dividends, buy back stock, invest in various types of acquisitions, invest excess funds (not immediately needed by the business), fund pension plans and pay interest and principal on the debt. One can see that with the myriad of sources and applications for cash and cash equivalents, the Finance function has a major, behind-the-scenes, dynamic orchestration job to do to permit the Momentum Maximizers and the Change Creators to "do their thing."

Since, to Finance, cash is king and the conservation one of cash their key roles, Finance is present wherever there are potential cash traps in the operation. Much attention has been paid recently to looking into ways to reduce "non-value-added" time spent by employees. Finance, for its part, is focused on minimizing "non-income- producing" tie ups of cash.

Receivables

One large cash trap is receivables. Once a good or service is shipped or delivered to a customer, all that cash in parts, labor and overhead costs that the company has invested in producing it, plus any cash profit to be received for providing it, is essentially invested in a receivable that ordinarily doesn't pay any interest. Small wonder that Finance focuses major attention on Accounts Receivable.

They measure themselves here on "day aging," always seeking ways to reduce the number of days the cash is "locked up" between delivery to the customer and receipt of payment. The Accounts Receivable people obviously must be good talkers, persuaders and facilitators for this job.

Customers (see discussion on payables) are obviously seeking ways to delay payment in any way they can. Any customer complaint on quality, performance or delivery is anathema to Accounts Receivable because it provides an excuse for withholding payment and the Momentum Maximizers involved usually immediately feel the heat.

Inventory

Another major lock up of cash is inventory. It is in this area that the people in Finance have had a major role in facilitating the great break-throughs in inventory reduction in the last few decades.

Recall that Finance pioneered the major involvement of computers in business and that typically the armies of programmers and computer operators initially required, all reported to Finance. (See section on Information Systems)

When Manufacturing Requirements Planning (MRP) techniques became available to Manufacturing, these systems required massive computer memory and processing capabilities, about which the Production people of the day knew little. The implementation of MRP and the latter refinements were made possible by a partnership of shared core competences between Finance's Information Systems (I/S) and Manufacturing. (In the early days, Manufacturing's dependence on the mainframe computer competence of Finance was so great that portions of I/S were drawn into a day-to-day operations mode). The Financial group, in addition, had to lay out the requirements as to which business information was to be available from the system and how the data was to be structured to be able to correctly, and promptly, pull information out. I/S (working with the manufacturing people installing the production scheduling portion) had to implement these requirements simultaneously.

The "early days" are way behind us (in the 2000's way of measuring time). We are now already beyond MRP II on our way to a completely PC based, networked system with no true "main frame." Even the earlier systems gave us, (for the first time), "reasonably" real- time data.... but, in many cases, too much of it. Newer programming technology permits "filtering" the mass of management data to display only the most meaningful data.

With the advent of convenient, user friendly, off-the-shelf software, the need for a large pool of in-house manufacturing systems programmers has diminished. Users have come to be able to rely on the "core competence" of the major software houses to keep updating to the newest capabilities.

Finance's support of Manufacturing's MRP, etc. (as part of their effort to reduce cash lock up) opened the door to double-digit inventory turns. Inventory turns are typically used as the index of success in reducing the inventory required supporting production. (Roughly, inventory turns is the ratio of the cost of goods sold for a rolling previous twelve month period divided by the inventory on hand at the time of the measurement).

The second largest pool of inventories, over that required to support production, are those for which Sales is normally held accountable. One of these is the finished goods inventory which is held at the main plant or dispersed warehouses (See "SALES") as a selling tool to help provide competitive deliveries, sometimes world wide. Another is the inventory of demonstration units (demos), controlled by sales, which are used to physically show the product and its performance to prospective buyers. Since all these pools are of final product with all the manufacturing cost, this is expensive inventory and Finance has to help sales by providing capital to fund it and financial information to support Sales in optimizing the commitment.

The last major potential inventory cash lock up is in spare parts. Depending on the type of product and any government regulatory or customer requirement, this can entail a considerable investment. It is one of the hardest to minimize (if one doesn't possess a time machine).

The best way to control and reduce the downstream investment in spare parts is to start out with a product structuring plan the day the company starts business and then make that plan part of the "Ten Commandments" under which future Change Creators must live. It is hard for Finance to make a case for spare (and renewal) parts investment reduction when there are customers that must be supported. If one attempts to charge for the spares the true cost of maintaining this "readiness to serve" capability, Sales would be impacted by customer reaction. (I tried to tell myself this story whenever I had to buy a part for my 1979 Mercedes but it still hurt).

Accounts Payable

One would think that in Accounts Payable the shoe would always be on the other foot compared to Accounts Receivable, and it is, with one major exception. That exception is the true supplier partner. Just as in a close alliance arrangement, competences are exchanged and incoming inspection eliminated so also is the receivable/payable game playing set aside. The two agree up front as to when cash will flow for the goods and services provided and both parties can exactly account and plan for the cash tie up necessary for the relationship.

In the non-partner payable situation, Accounts Payable must orchestrate the payments for goods and services to delay the outflow of cash as long as possible without upsetting the supplier relationship (or else paying early and taking a discount offered if that is more attractive).

Above all, Accounts Payable people must be good listeners because, if they're doing their job, they'll probably get lots of practice.

Payroll

Payroll is to a great extent considered "cut and dry" with little opportunity for creative changes. Good service by payroll is assumed and it is not considered by the employee as a positive, but lack of good service by payroll can be a strong employee negative. (Just let the checks be late and watch the employee non-value-added time meter go off scale.)

Capital Budgeting

Finance must provide input to help senior management referee the tug of war that goes on throughout the budgeting process and throughout the year between the Momentum Maximizers who want money to make capital investments to help the existing business and the Change Creators who want funding for new tooling for new products and processes.

Often the Senior Management of the company, based on the projections of Finance, will decide on a plan for a certain level of capital investment for the business year and/or the planning period. Considerations like depreciation allowances, net income expectations, return on asset targets all come into the calculation. If your Momentum Maximizers and Change Creators are "leaning forward in the traces" as they should be, the demand should far outstrip the proposed level and force healthy competition for the resources.

Treasurer

The Treasurer function sometimes comes under Finance and sometimes reports directly to Senior Management. My perception of this function is being concerned with tax planning as well as debt and equity funding, the two principle sources of cash that show on the balance sheet. The Treasurer arranges for the issuance and repurchase of all classes of stock as directed by Senior Management and required by the business. He arranges for any long term and short term debt required including lines of credit.

This individual, and the Senior Financial Executive, set up and maintain the relationships with the banks and other lending institutions that supply the major portion of the capital to most companies. The Treasurer quite frequently is also responsible for the investments the company makes to fund its pension program as well as investing any cash temporarily not required by operations, to earn interest.

It is usually the Treasurer, in partnership with Human Resources, who works on the funding and financial aspects of employee benefit plans. For example, this individual works with HR to set up retirees health plan arrangements. (See also discussion on benefits in Human Resources section).

Comptroller

We have previously touched on the comptroller's (controller's) role as the "Abbot of the Accountants." The comptroller also has a major role in aspects of providing support. As an example, working with the Information Systems people, comptrollers are now taking the lead in designing and implementing real time management information systems to allow all levels of management instant access to the data (with the accent on relevancy rather than quantity) they need to monitor and control their area of the operation. Even more sophisticated tools, with capabilities to extrapolate ahead and forecast potential problems (to provide "red lights") are being implemented.

This individual must provide the tools and information that the Momentum Maximizers (to some extent), the Change Creators (to a very great extent) and senior management need to evaluate the financial benefit/impact of any business proposal. For every administrative decision in the entire organization that requires financial data, it is the comptroller who sees that it is provided accurately and promptly. Plutarch observed, "When the candles are out, all women are fair." In business, the equivalent is that, when the numbers are sufficiently vague and obscure, any plan can look good. It is the Comptrollers role to "keep the candles lit."

LEGAL

As the most litigious society on the face of the earth, with probably the highest ratio of lawyers to population of any developed country, it is not surprising that every business must have all the major manifestations of legal support available at all times. Sometimes, there is in-house counsel as a coordinator, but most or all of the legal work is typically farmed out. Few manufacturing companies choose to have one of their "core competencies" to be a full range of capabilities in law. The principal exception is Patent Law, where the protection of intellectual property is such a major concern, particularly in the fast moving, high-tech businesses that firms may choose to staff this legal specialty internally.

When one thinks of it, it is amazing how many different kinds of law with which the corporation has to be prepared to deal. There is labor law, contract law (both union and inter-business), employee relations work (harassment, personal injury, discrimination, breach of employee/employer agreements of all types, etc.), environmental laws and regulations, patent & trademark, banking laws and regulations, estate (in family businesses), international, and on and on. Finding the right legal partner (or partners) to provide these competencies is every bit as important as identifying the right material or technology supplier partners.

COMMUNITY RELATIONS

The days when the mill owner lived in town "in the big house in the hill section" and the community could look to that individual for inter-face with the company are gone. The days when the community could expect the company to stay on in town, through good times and bad, but always somehow growing to provide jobs for the town kids graduat-ing from high school and college are gone as well.

To an increasing degree, due to the mergers and acquisitions that organizations have been forced into for survival or growth (or both), the plant in the town is typically now part of a larger corporation. Corporate headquarters are often "somewhere else."

To an increasing degree, due to the "re-engineering" and downsizing that organizations have been forced into for survival, the community has become suspicious of the company's statements and reassurances about the future. When the corporate headquarters are impersonally "somewhere else," distrust can deepen.

On the other hand, companies need the support of the communities in which they do business (even more than in the past) in providing the environment in which the plant functions. Good transportation, com-petitive taxes, education and training facilities (which in turn provide an adequate supply of motivated and skilled workers), water, sewage treatment, utilities, protection of property and personnel, reasonable environmental rules, modern building and zoning codes, high "quality of life" amenities (to help in attracting specialized skills to the area), fair treatment by the local media, are but a few of the company's needs, for which, the company looks to the community for satisfaction.

Into this dichotomy, from the company's side, moves the function typically identified as "Community Relations." As noted in the section on Senior Management, one of the roles of the President is to represent the company as a spokesperson to the community. In many far-flung companies this may be impractical at the local level and so the role falls to the highest ranked company official who is in residency, frequently a General Manager who may or may not bear the title Vice President. Since this individual typically has many other duties to perform, it is common for there to be individuals who do the staff work in this area.

If there are a number of different businesses of the company at a given location, it is not uncommon to have a "landlord" type organization that provides all the common support needs of the businesses. (See section on "Landlord Function") In that situation, it is natural for the community relations staff work to come under this umbrella. If there is only one business, then the Human Resources function of that business is likely as not to get the assignment.

Unfortunately, the squeeze to reduce costs often results in Community Relations only getting staff and senior management attention in a crisis. i.e., strike, layoffs, plant closing, utility outage, tax increase, etc. This is only after-the-fact damage control and understandably not as effective as it could be.

It would appear that it might be a good idea to approach the communities in which the company does business for the same two way "supplier partnership" relation the company is striving to attain with its suppliers of material and technology. From this perspective, perhaps Purchasing and Business Development ought to be brought more into the act of Community Relations strategy. It appears that corporate America could profitably invest more and different resources in an ongoing, growing partnership-style, Community Relations program, than it has in the recent past.

GOVERNMENT AND REGULATORY RELATIONS

As touched upon in the section on "Scorekeepers" there is an (apparently) ever increasing number of government agencies; federal, state and local (and more recently international agencies in such areas as quality control, intellectual property, etc.) Certain industries, such as health care, defense, and nuclear power have, in addition, a whole range of unique-to-the-industry regulatory bodies with which they must deal. In these industries, and to a lesser degree companies in other, less regulated, fields it has been found advisable to have an individual (with supporting staff if necessary), to manage the interface with these agencies.

We now see titles like "Vice President - Regulatory Affairs" cropping up on the organization charts of many companies. Since the cost of this additional overhead function must be passed on in the price of the product, it becomes one of the many hidden costs to our society for compliance with all these proliferating regulations. Like all the other Support activities, this organization provides the specialized assistance that the Momentum Maximizers and Change Creators need to help them get their job done, with a minimum of distraction.

The individuals normally selected to head up this activity must have a very specialized set of skills, experience, and credentials. The government officials with whom the VP - Regulatory Affairs and staff must deal with have no particular inherent interest in the profitability of the company/welfare of the stockholders or the importance of the employment base to the communities where the company operates. It is in the nature of bureaucrats to be risk adverse since, in their world, the consequences of "sticking ones neck out" in some approval or interpretation matter, that might conceivably have a bad outcome, are serious. To them, too often, the penalties for delay and rigidity, on the other hand, are virtually non-existent.

The regulatory affairs personnel of the company must therefore be skillful presenters, have authority of knowledge and experience sufficient to allay the technical concerns of the agency and above all, the rarest of all attributes, unquestioned credibility. This is hard enough when dealing with a few agencies, but the agency proliferation alluded to earlier have made it a Herculean task. As a result, many companies have been forced to spread out the interface assignment over a number of key individuals, each with specialized credentials in a particular agency specialty, with the regulatory affairs head as a team leader.

It occurred to me, as I wrote this, that here is another good argument for focusing on a few key competencies and the naturally related government regulatory bodies, and farming out to partners the other competencies and the regulatory interface that goes with them. A very visible example of this is the closing down of in-house foundries in companies who don't need "casting" as a core competence (and don't need the associated regulatory headaches associated with operating a foundry).

THE "LANDLORD" FUNCTIONS

In every manufacturing and/or office site there are a number of landlord type services that must be provided. Typical of these are facilities, security and utilities, which will be discussed below, but there are many more one can think of (fire protection, emergency medical capability, snow plowing, landscape maintenance, parking & traffic control, etc.). Since these capabilities are outside of those needed for the regular business, they are normally provided by some combination of specialized internal units and outside contractors. This "landlord" type support must be provided even though it is to some degree invisible to the Momentum Maximizers and Change Creators, who take it for granted.

It probably makes sense to group all these "landlord" functions under one individual who can be held accountable particularly if the company owns the property. In a lease situation, where there is an actual landlord, that person provides some of this support as part of the rent, and it may be possible to spread out the balance. The landlord function is kind of an orphan. Frequently it is placed under either Human Resources or Manufacturing (never Marketing or R.D.& E.) but it is somewhat diluent of the main mission of those functions. In these days of focus and core competence concentration, it may be best to consider farming the whole activity out to one outside contractor who specializes in providing landlord type services. Some major design/build firms are now offering to provide what amounts to a land-lord function for their clients.

Facilities

The basic jobs in this area haven't changed in many years. Construction of additional office or manufacturing space, building maintenance, painting, window cleaning, housekeeping and the like are traditional roles. What is new in this area relates to the impact of the Change Creators. Remaining competitive in the continually accelerating, global competition driven, business world today demands capability and flexibility in handling change. This means that not only the business have this capability but the facilities themselves as well.

It is no accident that industry has moved to such things as moveable partitions, modular furniture, ceiling-fed utilities and localizable lighting in the offices and to "minimally pillared" space and flexible worksta-tions in the factory. The facility must be structured to facilitate change in organization, process and product and the facilities people must be just as responsive to make the needed changes as the Change Creators them-selves must be in initiating the change. In taking maximum advantage of the capability provided by the flexible office and factory concepts, management has placed a major additional responsibility on the facilities function.

Security

In general, most companies find it desirable to farm out this particular specialty to an outside security firm. The most obvious reason is that, in times of labor unrest, you want the security force to be impartial and objective in protecting property and employees. There is however many other reasons for farm out. In modern times, security has become a much more complex activity. The major security firms have specialists that they can bring in to address problems like theft, sabotage, bomb threats, terrorism, etc. that are way outside the skills of the historic guard-gate organization. Even on such a mundane thing as access control, it is better to have a non-employee be the one to enforce identification and authorization rules.

Utilities

Just as in the facilities area, there are traditional roles for the utilities function i.e. electric power, gas, and telephone. The information age has heaped a whole new set of concerns on to the utilities people. Computers demand omnipresent cable connection to all the other information processing and storage facilities of the organization. There are specialized phone lines for high-speed data transmittal, microwave links, and satellite dishes. There must be "clean" (and occasionally uninterruptible) electric power provided to the computers and similar power quality sensitive equipment. In the space of a generation, "Utilities" have gone high tech!

SUMMARY AND INTRODUCTION TO THE POSTSCRIPTS

Whether you've plowed through, cherry picked or skimmed all the text that has gone before; I hope you have been able to see the validity of the concept. Momentum Maximization and Change Creation are going on all around us…in our personal lives, our governments, religious and secular organizations as well as in the business example cited here. It is a very useful tool for management.

When I read through what I have written, the core competence concept shows up as well, everywhere in the organization. That's all right because it too is a valuable management tool.

There were some subjects that I wanted to cover but could not find a way to work into the main text. One is the parallel between the content of this book and Chaos theory. Another is a discussion of the slow and steady approach to business success versus the "long bomb." I called it the business version of the parable of the Hare and the Tortoise. In addition, since the book utilizes a business organization to illustrate the concept, I have added a section that shows how it might apply in other types of organizations. These subjects are covered in the following Postscripts.

IX. CHANGE, MOMENTUM & CHAOS THEORY

It is with some trepidation that I inject some parallels from the broad subject of Chaos Theory to this discussion. In this particular area of technology, I see myself as very much an intellectual Gulliver entering into a field full of Brobdingnagian (mental) giants. Nevertheless, from the reading that I have done on the subject, I am struck by, what appears to me to be, direct parallels between the scenario in this book and some of the theories coming out of the Chaos work.

Could not business organizations, be considered examples of what is referred to in Chaos literature as "Complex Adaptive Systems?"

If one equates this text's Momentum to Chaos Theory's "Frozen State" and

If one equates this text's Change to "Chaos," then

Could not one then conclude that the business (system) that has successfully brought Change and Momentum into balance is therefore operating, to put it in Chaos Theory vernacular, "poised at the edge of chaos?"

Some chaos theorists feel that, in this position, i.e. poised at the edge of chaos, the system is at its state of maximum fitness, control and evolution readiness. In the world of business, empirical analysis of business results would appear to lead to the same conclusion.

As long as I have ventured (possibly over my head) into Chaos Theory, there is another analogy that struck me. Chaos theorists use a concept called fitness landscapes, which had apparently been initially proposed in the 1930s, by Sewell Wright, in the field of genetics. I'll quote the description from the book "Complexity" by Roger Lewin:

"…You have to think about the "fitness" of an individual in terms of different combinations of gene variants it might have. Now think of a landscape, in which each different point on the landscape represents slightly different packages of these variants. Lastly, if you imagine some of these packages as being fitter than others, raise them up as peaks. The fittest of the packages has the highest peak. The landscape overall will be rugged, with peaks of different height, separated by valleys. Remember, this landscape represents fitness probabilities, places where individuals of a species might be, depending on the combination of genetic variants they have in their chromosomes. If an individual happens to be in a fitness valley, then mutation and selection might push it up to a local peak, representing a rise in fitness. Once on the local peak it may, metaphorically, gaze enviously at a nearby peak, but be unable to reach it because that would involve crossing a valley of lower fitness."

WOW! It's the core competence concept all over again, only this time coming at it from the science of genetics, and further expanded by the chaos theorists. The analogy appears to have fascinating possibilities for expanding the vista of, and perhaps applying other scientific theory to, the study of core competence in the business field.

X. THE TORTOISE AND THE HARE (BUSINESS VERSION)

(or the "Ground Game" versus the "Long Bomb")

The reality of the Tortoise and Hare Race is that, if it were run over and over, some times the Hare would win and probably "win big." (Slow and steady doesn't always win the race.)The reality of football is that most "drives" are steady ground games…involving running and short passes (with high completion and low interception probability). Once in a while, however, the long bomb, or so-called "Hail Mary" forward pass, is completed, for a dramatic touchdown!

Business has the same dichotomy.

If one runs the business carefully and conservatively, seeking opportunities, building and expanding into technologies that are peripheral to the business's core competency technologies, into distribution channels that are similar to the existing core distribution, into processes that are similar to the existing core process capabilities, etc. strong, sustainable growth can be achieved…say for instance 15% per year in constant dollars. In my view, most companies that succeed follow this formula. It involves slugging it out, market-by-market, million by million, using the "ground game," the slow-and-steady-wins-the-race formula of the tortoise …and it works well.

Many companies and individuals have thrown "long bombs" in the history of American business. Individuals such as Thomas Edison, Henry Ford, Andrew Carnegie and more recently Ross Perot and Bill Gates can perhaps be cited as examples of those who pulled it off. In the corporate area, GE's synthetic industrial diamond and Bell Labs transistor are shining examples. However, the majority of those who tried this approach have failed and history seldom even recalls their name (well, maybe some people remember Tucker).

Paradoxically however, the few "long bomb" throwers who do succeed have usually brought about the great leaps forward in business, the paradigm shifts. It is their incredible optimism, in the face of long odds, it is their willingness to jump into areas where there is little if any "competency support" to fall back on, that can bring about dramatic success and dramatic change. The hidden costs are the destroyed companies and careers of the majority of those who gambled and lost with this strategy.

Military history is replete with examples of these strategies. Washington's attack on Trenton was certainly a classic "long bomb." During the Second World War, the war in the Pacific was being fought as a "ground game" slugging it out island by island until a "long bomb" (in this case an actual bomb) abruptly ended the war. England's attempts to relieve Norway at Narvik or to defend Greece in 1941 could be viewed as military "long bombs" that failed.

Just as a quarterback, battered by the punishing work of slugging it out, yard by yard, longs to throw that one long, magnificent pass that wins the game, so the CEO of a modestly successful corporation may long for that big gamble that could put his (and his company's) name in the "big winners" circle.

Does the "long bomb" ever make business sense? Here are two straightforward scenarios where it does. Interestingly, in both these cases it makes sense because it doesn't matter if the attempt fails.... but for different reasons.

The first, and most obvious case study is when the business is "going down the tubes" anyhow...the "ground game" has failed. Whether it is due to factors within or not within the organization's control makes little difference at this point. One might as well gamble on a bold move...a long shot. In Hollywood movies this tactic always saves the show or the company or the battle. In real business life it works only once in a while, but if one has nothing more to lose if it fails…why not?

The quote that to me typifies this case was the statement of Marshall Foch at the Second Battle of the Marne in WWI. He said:

"Mon centre cede,
(My center is giving way)
ma droite recule,
(My right is pushed back)
j'attaque."
(I attack)

Another situation in which the "long bomb" could be used (but where it is probably too infrequently applied) is when the base business, playing its "ground game," is so strong that the consequences of the gamble failing would not have a significant impact upon it. These are situations where the CEO has an opportunity to make a rising star company into a shooting star company, without even having to "bet the ranch."

One of the reasons this second opportunity for a dramatic breakout is not seized is the reluctance of many CEOs to risk being personally identified with a plan or strategy that failed, no matter why it failed. For this reason, it is easier for the actual owners of businesses to stick their necks out than it is for hired management.

Another reason for not using this strategy is that the management team in place, throughout the organization, which has been fine tuned to win at the "ground game" may not have the personalities and entrepreneurial skills needed for high risk beachhead establishment work. Once again, the CEO must stick his neck out and keep in the organization enough "lean and hungry" risk preferrers to staff the occasional major preemptive strike. This task if further complicated by the natural hostility toward these "mavericks" from the rest of the organization, who are fighting the good fight and "taking care of business."

It is a mistake to assume that the main stream of the Change Creators themselves welcome the "long bomb" throwers with open arms. Even to the Change Creators, these folks are the equivalent of extreme, radical right wingers (or left wingers) whose "fly by night" schemes are viewed as diverting resources and attention from the real work of growing the business. If it is desirable to maintain a team for high-risk gambles in new areas, senior management must protect, nurture and motivate these people…their peers will "devour" them if given a chance.

There is one other occasion that occurs to me where the "long bomb" may make sense in a business situation, but it is from a slightly different perspective. There are situations where a company, operating primarily in a market that is currently "out of favor" with the financial analysts and other stock market gurus, wishes to raise equity cash through an IPO. In this instance, I have seen companies (prior to the IPO and on a highly publicized basis) make acquisitions in, or enter by other means, markets or product areas that are somewhat foreign to their base business, but which are "hot" areas in the eyes of the stock market players.

This may appear cynical but the hard fact is that, if the financial benefit in helping the placement succeed is significantly greater than the downside cost should the "long bomb" fail, the move could be considered to make business sense. On the other hand, if, in spite of all the odds, the "long bomb" succeeds, one has a win-win situation.

To those who might feel that this borders on chicanery, it might help to consider that the valuation of all publicly traded stocks is built upon perception, first of what seems to have happened to a particular company and its market in the past and then of what seems likely to happen (or appear to happen) in the future. We dress up brides, fully knowing that they will not go through the rest of their lives in a long white dress with a lace train. Is it necessarily inappropriate to dress up an otherwise somewhat dowdy company with a white dress in the form of a "long bomb" to make it more attractive?

XI. CHANGE AND MOMENTUM IN GOVERMENT, EDUCATION, RELIGIOUS INSTITUTIONS AND THE MILITARY

The author does not have the depth of experience in these areas to enable an organizational component by component analysis, like that performed on the typical manufacturing company organization used as an example in the body of this book. Instead some general, possible assignment of roles in these organizations will be proposed to illustrate how the Change Creation and Momentum Maximization concept might be applied.

A. Government

In a typical Parliamentary type of government there are three branches: the Legislative, the Judicial and the Executive. The Legislative branch may be considered as primarily a Change Creation activity. It is engaged in passing new laws or repealing old laws thereby changing the way that the government operates. There are usually some committees within the Legislative branch whose role is that of Score Keepers, particularly in the measurement of the activities and performance of the Executive branch. There is also a certain degree of Momentum Maximization related to the task of getting re-elected, which in some situations like the U. S. House of Representatives, appears to take entirely too much time away from the basic "Legislative" role.

The Judiciary ought to be purely a Momentum Maximization role. Unfortunately, in situations where the Legislative branch passes confusing or incomplete legislation, the Judiciary, through the vehicle of "interpretation," may actually be participating in Change Creation. This is clearly an undesirable situation.

The Executive branch should be primarily a Momentum Maximization activity, acting as the steward in operating the government for the benefit of the people in the most efficient manner possible under the existing laws. Long range planning and budgeting activities have a Change Creator focus but they consume a very small part of the Executive branch resource. The Executive branch also furnishes Support and Score Keeping services to all three branches and thereby to the Change Creators and Momentum Maximizers contained therein.

B. Education

The great danger in Education would seem to be that the Momentum Maximizers become so strong and entrenched that the necessary process of Change Creation may be stifled. The great institutions of higher learning, that have continued to lead over long periods, seem to be those where a certain amount of controversy and unrest among students and faculty has occurred on a regular basis over the years.

C. Religious Institutions

Historically, religious institutions appear to have a unique approach to Change Creation. Day to day operations are strongly focused on Momentum Maximization, sometimes for many years. During these periods, theologians are busy discussing new insights and pressure from changes that are occurring in society in general, is increasing. In these times, early, vocal Change Creators (including prophets) are often harshly dealt with. Then, just before (or sometimes just after) the theological or social "pot boil over" a council or conference or convocation is called and the Change Creators have their opportunity to make the adjustments required to restore the vitality of the particular faith, denomination or sect. All that has been discussed earlier, including Chaos Theory, would predict that the religious organization without controversy is doomed to extinction.

D. The Military

One could make the case that those in the military who were focused on "Attack" and "Assault" are Change Creators and perhaps should approach their task with that mindset. Those whose role is "Defense" are by nature Momentum Maximizers with that mindset. The Support Suppliers are perhaps more explicitly identified in military organizations than in any other type of organization. With so much pressure to put the right spin on results, the job of Score Keeping in the military is difficult to say the least.

Bibliography

Barnard, Chester. *The Functions of the Executive*. Harvard University Press, 1938.

Carroll, Lewis. *Alice's Adventures in Wonderland and Through the Looking Glass*. Macmillan, 1963.

Coventry, William and Irving Burstiner. *Management - A Basic Handbook*. Prentice-Hall, 1977.

Encyclopedia Britannica. 15th Edition. s.v. "Accounting."

Fromm, Erich. *Escape from Freedom*. Rinehart, 1941.

Hamel, Gary and C.K. Prahalad. *Competing for the Future*. Harvard Business School Press, 1994.

Lewin, Roger. Complexity - *Life at the Edge of Chaos*. Macmillan, 1992.

Machiavelli, Nicolo. *The Prince*. (1513) trans. by W. K. Marriott. Encyclopedia Britannica, 1952. (Derived from the edition in Everyman's Library, J. M. Dent & Sons, London and E. P. Dutton, New York).

Pareto, Vilfredo. *The Mind and Society*. Harcourt, Brace, 1935.

Selznick, Philip. *Leadership in Administration*. Univ. of So. California Press, 1957.

Tzu, Sun. *The Art of War*. (300 or 500 BC) trans. by Lionel Giles. Delacorte Press, 1983.

Articles

Hamel, Gary and C. K. Prahalad. *The Core Competency of the Corporation*. Harvard Business Review May-June 1990 pgs. 79-91.

Hamel, Gary and C. K. Prahalad. *Strategic Intent*. Harvard Business Review May-June 1989 pgs. 63-76.

Miller, William R. *Engineering Productivity Can Be Measured*. Machine Design, October 28, 1971 pgs.72-76.

Index